Liferay Portal Performance Best Practices

A practical tutorial to learn the best practices for building high performing Liferay-based solutions

Samir Bhatt

BIRMINGHAM - MUMBAI

Liferay Portal Performance Best Practices

Copyright © 2013 Packt Publishing

All rights reserved. No part of this book may be reproduced, stored in a retrieval system, or transmitted in any form or by any means, without the prior written permission of the publisher, except in the case of brief quotations embedded in critical articles or reviews.

Every effort has been made in the preparation of this book to ensure the accuracy of the information presented. However, the information contained in this book is sold without warranty, either express or implied. Neither the author, nor Packt Publishing, and its dealers and distributors will be held liable for any damages caused or alleged to be caused directly or indirectly by this book.

Packt Publishing has endeavored to provide trademark information about all of the companies and products mentioned in this book by the appropriate use of capitals. However, Packt Publishing cannot guarantee the accuracy of this information.

First published: June 2013

Production Reference: 1030613

Published by Packt Publishing Ltd.
Livery Place
35 Livery Street
Birmingham B3 2PB, UK.

ISBN 978-1-78216-368-8

www.packtpub.com

Cover Image by Faiz Fattohi (faizfattohi@gmail.com)

Credits

Author
Samir Bhatt

Reviewers
Gaurav Barot
Albert Coronado Calzada
Chintan Mehta

Acquisition Editor
Kartikey Pandey

Commissioning Editor
Harsha Bharwani

Technical Editors
Jalasha D'costa
Amit Ramadas

Project Coordinator
Sneha Modi

Proofreader
Maria Gould

Indexer
Hemangini Bari

Graphics
Abhinash Sahu

Production Coordinator
Aditi Gajjar

Cover Work
Aditi Gajjar

About the Author

Samir Bhatt is an Enterprise Architect with over 12 years of IT experience. He has been working on Liferay-Portal-based solutions for the last four years. He has co-authored a book, *Liferay Beginner's Guide* by *Packt Publishing*. He is also a Liferay certified trainer and has delivered public and private training across the world. Samir leads an architectural group at CIGNEX Datamatics. He extensively worked on performance tuning of Liferay-Portal-based solutions. Apart from Liferay Portal, Samir has also worked on many other technologies and frameworks including Hadoop, MongoDB, Pentaho BI, Oracle, Java Swing, ICEfaces, ZK, Spring, Hibernate, and Visual Basic.

Samir is also a very good speaker and has delivered various webinars on Liferay, Pentaho BI, and MongoDB. He blogs at `www.connect-sam.com`.

> I would like to specially thank my mentor and CTO of CIGNEX Datamatics, Munwar Sharif, for encouraging me to write this book.
>
> I sincerely thank the entire Packt Publishing team for providing continuous support throughout this project.
>
> Last but not least, I would like to give a big thanks to my parents, my wife Hetal, and my little daughter Shreeya for supporting and encouraging me throughout the project.

About the Reviewers

Gaurav Barot is a Liferay Architect having 8 years of industry experience, with more than 4 years of experience in Liferay Portal technologies. He has executed Liferay projects in various domains such as media, healthcare, insurance, and so on. He has been involved in the complete life cycle of the project starting from requirement gathering to deployment. He has worked on various versions of Liferay from 5.x to 6.1. He is a certified trainer as well and has provided more than 15 successful private and public training sessions to more than 100 trainees across the globe.

He works with CIGNEX Datamatics, which is a global leader in Open Source technologies. He leads Liferay Practice having nearly 200 members at his organization. Gaurav also co-authored *Liferay Beginner's Guide* by *Packt Publishing*.

> I would like to thank my parents and my two younger sisters, Kinjal and Yogini, for their love and encouragement. A special thanks to my wife Kruti and my lovely daughter Twisha; both of them have been very tolerant and understanding during all the time I've spent on the computer while reviewing this book.

Albert Coronado Calzada is a highly experienced IT professional with more than 13 years of experience in Java EE, high performance portals, e-commerce, and enterprise software solutions. Albert has completed his Engineering degree in Information Technology and has pursued a Master's in Economic and Financial Management of Companies.

Albert is currently working as a freelance software developer, technical trainer, and consultant for international customers. Albert is an open source software contributor and has released different applications for Liferay and Android.

Albert has also worked on *Liferay Beginner's Guide* and *Instant Liferay Portal 6 Starter* by *Packt Publishing*.

Albert lives in Girona (Spain) and maintains a blog at http://www.albertcoronado.com. You can contact him through Linkedin (es.linkedin.com/in/albertcoronado/) or Twitter (@acoronadoc).

Chintan Mehta has over 10 years of progressive experience in Systems and Server Administration of Linux and open source technologies, along with applications such as Liferay, Alfresco, Drupal, Moodle, Magento, and Compiere. While developing his expertise in these areas, he also enhanced his technical skills in database administration, security, and performance tuning. He heads the Managed Cloud Services practice at CIGNEX Datamatics, and is involved in creating solutions and consulting customers on the cloud. Chintan has done Diploma in Computer Hardware and has a Network certification from a reputed institute in India.

www.PacktPub.com

Support files, eBooks, discount offers and more

You might want to visit www.PacktPub.com for support files and downloads related to your book.

Did you know that Packt offers eBook versions of every book published, with PDF and ePub files available? You can upgrade to the eBook version at www.PacktPub.com and as a print book customer, you are entitled to a discount on the eBook copy. Get in touch with us at service@packtpub.com for more details.

At www.PacktPub.com, you can also read a collection of free technical articles, sign up for a range of free newsletters and receive exclusive discounts and offers on Packt books and eBooks.

http://PacktLib.PacktPub.com

Do you need instant solutions to your IT questions? PacktLib is Packt's online digital book library. Here, you can access, read and search across Packt's entire library of books.

Why Subscribe?

- Fully searchable across every book published by Packt
- Copy and paste, print and bookmark content
- On demand and accessible via web browser

Free Access for Packt account holders

If you have an account with Packt at www.PacktPub.com, you can use this to access PacktLib today and view nine entirely free books. Simply use your login credentials for immediate access.

Table of Contents

Preface — 1

Chapter 1: Architectural Best Practices — 7

  The Liferay Portal reference architecture — 7
    The Presentation tier — 9
    The Networking tier — 9
    The Web tier — 9
    The Application tier — 9
    The Database Repository tier — 10
    The Search Repository tier — 10
    The Media Repository tier — 10
    The Active Directory tier — 10
    Reference architecture characteristics — 10
      Scalability — 11
      Performance — 11
      High availability and fault tolerance — 11
      Security — 11
  The Deployment sizing approach — 12
    The reference hardware — 13
    The performance benchmark test summary — 14
    An example of sizing calculations — 15
      Sample performance requirements — 15
      Sizing calculations — 15
  The Documents and Media Library architecture — 15
    File System and Advanced File System stores — 16
    The Database store — 16
    The JCR store — 17
    The CMIS store — 17
    The S3 store — 18
  The database architecture — 18
    The read/write database — 18

Database sharding	19
Static content delivery	**20**
Content Delivery Network	21
Content delivery through the web server	21
The caching architecture	**22**
Caching using Ehcache	22
Ehcache replication using RMI	22
Ehcache replication using Cluster Link	23
Caching using Terracotta	24
Web resource caching using Varnish	25
The search architecture	**26**
Apache Lucene	26
Index storage on SAN	26
Lucene Index replication using Cluster Link	27
Apache Solr	27
Summary	**29**
Chapter 2: Load Balancing and Clustering Best Practices	**31**
The basics of load balancing and clustering with Liferay	**32**
Setting up Liferay Portal nodes	**33**
Software load balancer configuration using the Apache Web Server	**35**
Load balancer configuration using mod_jk	35
Load balancer configuration using mod_proxy_ajp	37
Load balancer configuration using mod_proxy_http	39
Load balancing best practices	41
Liferay Portal cluster configuration	**41**
Session replication configuration	42
Cache replication	44
Ehcache replication using RMI	45
Ehcache configuration using JGroups	46
Ehcache replication using Cluster Links	47
Ehcache clustering best practices	47
Media Library configuration	48
Network file storage using the Advanced File System store	48
Database storage using the JCR store	49
Database storage using DBStore	52
Media Library clustering best practices	52
Search engine configuration	53
Lucene index storage on network storage	53
Lucene index replication using Cluster Link	54
Using the Apache Solr search engine	54
Clustering best practices for the search engine	56
Quartz scheduler configuration	56
Summary	**57**

Chapter 3: Configuration Best Practices — 59
Liferay Portal configuration best practices — 60
Servlet filter configuration — 60
- The auto login filter — 60
- The CAS filter — 61
- The NTLM SSO filter — 61
- The OpenSSO filter — 61
- The SharePoint filter — 62
- The GZip filter — 62
- The Strip filter — 62
- The ValidHtml filter — 63

Auto login hooks — 63
Counter increment — 63
User session tracker — 64
Direct Servlet Context — 64
Plugin repositories — 65
Pingbacks and trackbacks — 65
Google's blog search ping integration — 66
- The asset view counter — 66
- Document ranks and view count — 66
- Scheduler configuration — 67
- Inline permission checks — 69
- Lucene Configuration — 70

Application Server configuration best practices — 70
Database connection pool configuration — 70
JVM configuration — 72
- Garbage Collection — 72
- The Java Heap configuration — 73

JSP engine configuration — 74
Thread pool configuration — 75

Apache Web Server configuration best practices — 76
Static content delivery — 76
GZip compression configuration — 78
Cache header configuration — 79
Apache Web Server MPM configuration — 80

Summary — 81

Chapter 4: Caching Best Practices — 83
Customizing the Ehcache configuration — 83
Hibernate Ehcache CacheManager — 85
Single-VM CacheManager — 86
Multi-VM CacheManager — 86

Ehcache configuration best practices — 86
Caching using Terracotta — 89
Summary — 92

Chapter 5: Development Best Practices — 93
UI best practices — 93
Reducing the number of JavaScript files — 94
Reducing the number of CSS files — 96
Using CSS image sprites — 96
Minifying JavaScript files — 98
JavaScript positioning — 99
Limiting the use of DOM operations — 100
Analyzing web page performance using tools — 100
Portlet development best practices — 101
Limiting the use of dynamic queries — 101
Liferay caching API — 102
Coding best practices — 103
Summary — 103

Chapter 6: Load Testing and Performance Tuning — 105
Getting ready for load testing — 106
Capturing load testing requirements — 106
Selecting load testing tools — 107
- Apache JMeter — 107
- BlazeMeter — 107
- Apache Benchmark (ab) — 108

Preparing load testing scripts — 108
Setting up the load testing environment — 110
Conducting load tests — 110
Resource monitoring and performance tuning — 111
Liferay Portal server – monitoring and tuning — 111
- JConsole — 111
- VisualVM — 113
- JVM – monitoring and tuning — 114
- Tomcat thread – monitoring and tuning — 117
- Database connection pool – monitoring and tuning — 119
- Cache – monitoring and tuning — 121

Apache web server – monitoring and tuning — 123
Monitoring the database server — 124
- CPU and memory usage — 124
- Slow queries — 124
- Connections — 125
- Lock monitoring — 125

Monitoring logfiles — 125
Summary — 126

Index — 127

Preface

Liferay is the most popular portal based on open standards, written in Java. It was named Leader in Gartner's Magic Quadrant for Horizontal Portals. Many influential sites have been implemented with or have switched to Liferay Portal. The Liferay platform is highly scalable to serve millions of pages to millions of users on all web browsers, tablets, and mobile devices. We, at CIGNEX Datamatics, have implemented more than 200 large enterprise portals using Liferay since 2006. I was leading Liferay Practice at CIGNEX Datamatics with a staff of 240 Liferay experts. We have tuned many Liferay-based sites, and also trained many administrators and developers in Liferay. This book distills the hands-on approach of my project engagements into a concise, practical book.

Liferay Portal Performance Best Practices will explain to you how to implement high-performing, Liferay-based solutions by following various best practices. The book not only explains the best practices in detail, but also provides the detailed instructions to implement them. By following the logical flow of the chapters, you will learn performance-related best practices that should be followed during the architecture, design, development, deployment, and testing phases. You will also learn best practices for conducting performance tuning activities for a Liferay-based solution. By the end of this book you will have the advanced knowledge to implement a high-performing, Liferay-based solution.

What this book covers

Chapter 1, Architectural Best Practices, talks about the Liferay Portal reference architecture. It talks about various architectural options for implementing high-performing, Liferay-based solutions.

Chapter 2, Load Balancing and Clustering Best Practices, teaches you how to implement load balancing and clustering for a Liferay-based solution. It teaches you about various configuration options for implementing clustering.

Chapter 3, Configuration Best Practices, teaches you various configurations for improving performance of Liferay-based solutions. It talks about performance-related configuration options for the Apache web server, the Tomcat server, Liferay Portal, and so on.

Chapter 4, Caching Best Practices, talks about various options related to caching for improving the performance of Liferay-based solutions. It also teaches you how to configure Liferay Portal with the Terracotta cache server.

Chapter 5, Development Best Practices, talks about some of the key Liferay-specific development practices for developing a high-performing, Liferay-based solution.

Chapter 6, Load Testing and Performance Tuning, teaches you how to perform load testing and performance tuning exercises for a Liferay-based solution. It talks about best practices and guidelines related to load testing and performance tuning. It talks about how to monitor various resources during a load testing exercise in order to fine-tune the solution.

What you need for this book

The following is the software that you will need for *Liferay Portal Performance Best Practices*.

- Liferay Portal 6.1 CE GA2 Tomcat Bundle (http://downloads.sourceforge.net/project/lportal/Liferay%20Portal/6.1.1%20GA2/liferay-portal-tomcat-6.1.1-ce-ga2-20120731132656558.zip)
- Apache Web Server 2.x (http://httpd.apache.org/download.cgi)
- MySQL Community Server 5.5.29 (http://dev.mysql.com/downloads/)
- Terracotta Server Array, with Ehcache and Quartz (http://terracotta.org/downloads/open-source/destination?name=terracotta-3.7.5-installer.jar&bucket=tcdistributions&file=terracotta-3.7.5-installer.jar)

Who this book is for

Developers and architects who already work on Liferay Portal will find this book very useful. Also, system administrators who administer Liferay-Portal-based solutions will find this book very useful.

Conventions

In this book, you will find a number of styles of text that distinguish between different kinds of information. Here are some examples of these styles, and an explanation of their meaning.

Code words in text are shown as follows: "Instead of using `SingleVMPoolUtil`, we will need to use the `MultiVMPoolUtil` class to store and retrieve objects from the cache."

A block of code is set as follows:

```
/arrows/01_down.png=0,16,16
/arrows/01_left.png=16,16,16
/arrows/01_right.png=32,16,16
/arrows/01_up.png=48,16,16
```

When we wish to draw your attention to a particular part of a code block, the relevant lines or items are set in bold:

```
package com.connectsam.development;

import com.liferay.portal.kernel.cache.SingleVMPoolUtil;
import java.util.ArrayList;
import java.util.List;

public class SingleVMPoolExample {
  public List<String> getTestList(String key){
    List<String> listOfStrings = null;
```

New terms and **important words** are shown in bold. Words that you see on the screen, in menus or dialog boxes for example, appear in the text like this: "In JConsole, navigate to the **MBeans** tab and then expand **net.sf.ehcache | CacheStatistics | liferay-multi-vm-clustered**."

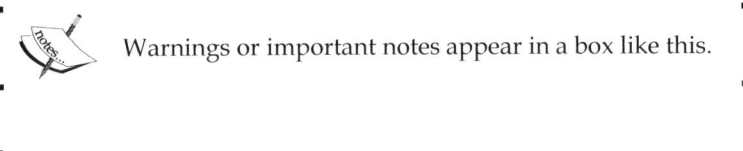

Warnings or important notes appear in a box like this.

Tips and tricks appear like this.

Reader feedback

Feedback from our readers is always welcome. Let us know what you think about this book—what you liked or may have disliked. Reader feedback is important for us to develop titles that you really get the most out of.

To send us general feedback, simply send an e-mail to feedback@packtpub.com, and mention the book title via the subject of your message.

If there is a topic that you have expertise in and you are interested in either writing or contributing to a book, see our author guide on www.packtpub.com/authors.

Customer support

Now that you are the proud owner of a Packt book, we have a number of things to help you to get the most from your purchase.

Errata

Although we have taken every care to ensure the accuracy of our content, mistakes do happen. If you find a mistake in one of our books—maybe a mistake in the text or the code—we would be grateful if you would report this to us. By doing so, you can save other readers from frustration and help us improve subsequent versions of this book. If you find any errata, please report them by visiting http://www.packtpub.com/submit-errata, selecting your book, clicking on the **errata submission form** link, and entering the details of your errata. Once your errata are verified, your submission will be accepted and the errata will be uploaded on our website, or added to any list of existing errata, under the Errata section of that title. Any existing errata can be viewed by selecting your title from http://www.packtpub.com/support.

Piracy

Piracy of copyright material on the Internet is an ongoing problem across all media. At Packt, we take the protection of our copyright and licenses very seriously. If you come across any illegal copies of our works, in any form, on the Internet, please provide us with the location address or website name immediately so that we can pursue a remedy.

Please contact us at copyright@packtpub.com with a link to the suspected pirated material.

We appreciate your help in protecting our authors, and our ability to bring you valuable content.

Questions

You can contact us at questions@packtpub.com if you are having a problem with any aspect of the book, and we will do our best to address it.

1
Architectural Best Practices

The most important aspect that affects the performance of a system is architecture. It is often seen that systems fails to perform as expected because of wrong architectural decisions. Liferay is a leading open source platform for developing high-performing portals. In this chapter, we will focus on the architecture of Liferay-Portal-based solutions. We will learn about various aspects which should be considered while defining the architecture of a Liferay-based solution. By the end of this chapter, we will learn about:

- The Liferay Portal reference architecture
- The Deployment sizing approach
- Documents and Media Library architecture options
- Database architecture options
- Architectural options for handling static resources
- Caching architecture options
- Search engine architecture options

The Liferay Portal reference architecture

Defining the architecture of a system from scratch requires an enormous amount of effort for researching, investigating, and taking right architectural decisions. We can reduce the effort by referring to the reference architecture for similar kinds of solutions. We can also ensure including a set of architectural best practices from the reference architecture. In this section, we will talk about the reference architecture of Liferay-Portal-based solution. This reference architecture can be used as a base for any Liferay-Portal-based portal solution. Of course, necessary changes have to be made in the reference architecture depending upon specific requirements. The rest of the chapter will help Liferay architects to make the right architectural decisions for such changes.

Architectural Best Practices

Here is the reference architecture diagram of Liferay-Portal-based solution:

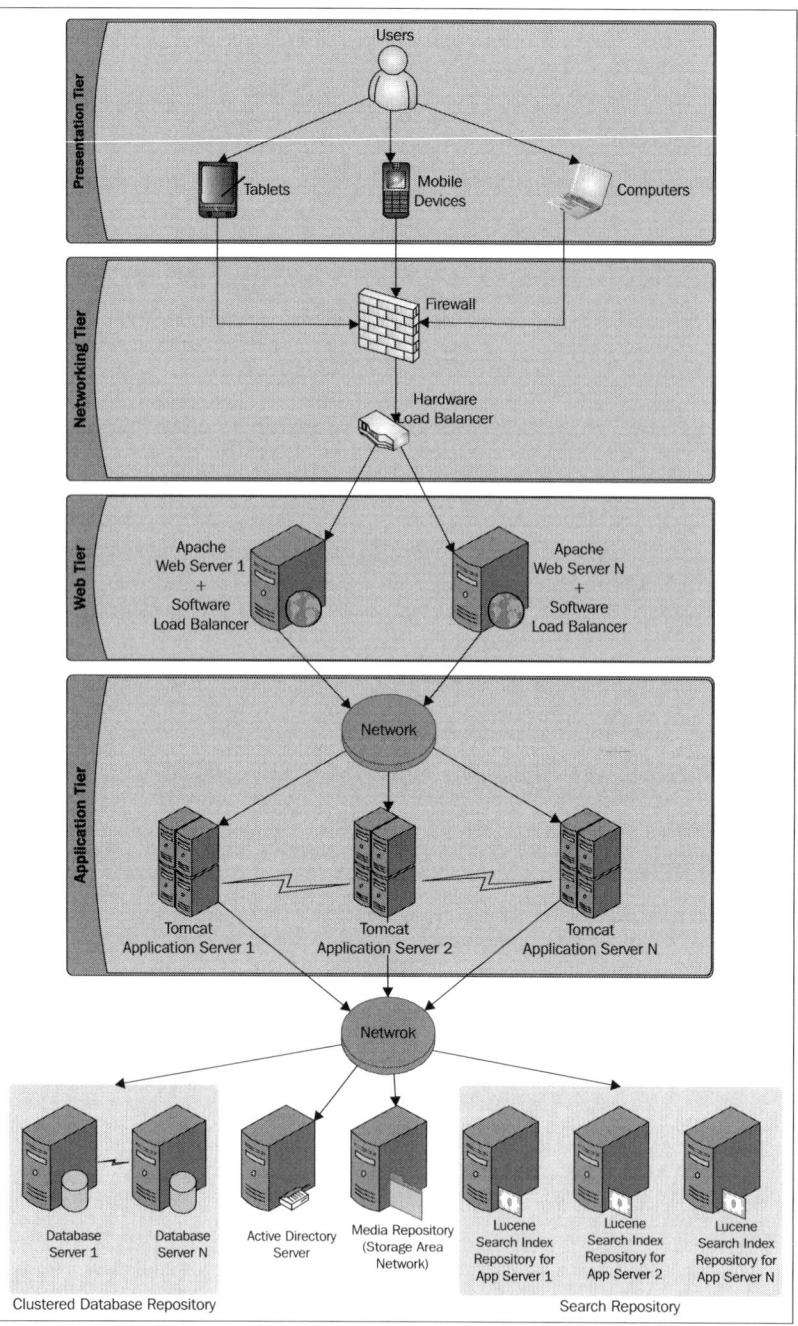

The Presentation tier

As shown in the previous diagram, users of the portal will access the Portal using tablets, mobile devices, or through PC browsers. Liferay Portal 6.1 supports various devices, and we won't need any special component to render content for mobile devices. Liferay Portal can even detect specific devices and respond with device-specific content. Liferay also supports creating responsive web design using its UI framework called **AlloyUI**.

The Networking tier

As shown in the reference architecture, every request will pass through Firewall. Firewall will filter unsecure requests. All valid user requests will be passed to the Hardware Load Balancer. The hardware load balancer is a hardware appliance which distributes loads between multiple web servers. The hardware load balancer can also deal with the failure of web servers. In case a of failure of any web server, the hardware load balancer diverts traffic to working web servers. There are a number of hardware load balancers available on the market. Some of the popular hardware load balancer vendors include F5, Cisco, Radware, CoyotePoint, and Barracuda.

The Web tier

The Web tier includes a series of Apache Web Servers. As shown in the reference architecture diagram, each Web Server is connected with each Application Server. The Web Server acts as a Software Load Balancer for Application Servers. Web servers can also act as components to serve static resources. The Apache Web Server connects with the Liferay Portal application server using `mod_jk`, `mod_proxy`, or `mod_proxy_ajp` connectors. These are popular connecters available with the Apache Web Server.

The Application tier

The Application tier includes one or more Liferay Portal application servers. Liferay Portal can be deployed on many different application servers. The reference architecture recommends using the most popular Apache Tomcat Server. Application servers are connected with web servers using the AJP protocol or the HTTP protocol. As shown in the diagram, there is a communication link between Application Servers. Each Application Server is connected with other Application Servers to replicate the session information, and cache and/or search indexes. Each Application Server is connected to dedicated Database Servers and Active Directory Servers.

The Database Repository tier

The Liferay Portal server connects to the Database Repository tier. For production systems, it is advisable to set up multiple database instances with replication. Such a setup ensures high availability of Database Servers. Liferay Portal works with majority of open source and propriety databases. In our reference architecture, we will use MySQL, which is one of the popular open source databases.

The Search Repository tier

Liferay Portal comes with an embedded Apache Lucene search engine. The Lucene search engine stores search indexes in a filesystem. As shown in the reference architecture diagram, each Application Server has its own search index repository in the Search Repository tier. Search engine repositories can be synchronized by the Liferay Portal server using the Cluster Link feature.

The Media Repository tier

Liferay Portal comes with a media repository, which includes a document library, image gallery, and so on. Liferay Portal provides different options to store the media repository content. By default, Liferay stores the media repository content on a filesystem. It can be configured to store the media repository content on a **database**, **Java Content Repository (JCR)**, **CMIS-based repository**, or **Amazon S3**. As shown in the reference architecture diagram, we have used a centralized filesystem to store the media repository content. To avoid issues related to concurrent access on a centralized filesystem, it is recommended to use **Storage Area Network** (**SAN**) as the centralized filesystem to store the Media Library content.

The Active Directory tier

Liferay comes with its own user repository. Liferay maintains its user repository in a database. But for production systems, it is recommended to integrate the user repository with identity management systems. The reference architecture refers using the Active Directory server. Liferay Portal connects with the Active Directory Server using the LDAP protocol.

Reference architecture characteristics

In the previous section, we learned about various tiers of the reference architecture. Let's understand how the reference architecture addresses architectural concerns.

Scalability

As shown in the architecture diagram, horizontal scaling is used for both the Web tier and the Application tier. Most of the components in the architecture are decoupled and hence if the user base is increased, we can scale up by adding extra nodes. We can establish linear scalability of the solution by using a performance benchmarking exercise. This can enable us to increase the capacity of the system by increasing 'x' number of Liferay application servers, web servers, or database servers.

Performance

The reference architecture divides the load of the system to multiple tiers. A static resource's requests can be served by the Web tier directly. Also, the Web tier is load balanced using the Hardware Load Balancer. So, the load on each web server is also controlled. Similarly, all application requests will be served by the clustered Application Server tier. The Application Server connects with the Database tier which is again clustered to ensure the load is distributed. The reference architecture ensures that the architecture of the solution is robust enough for delivering high performance.

High availability and fault tolerance

The reference architecture ensures that the most important tiers of the solutions are clustered and load balanced to ensure that the system is highly available and fault tolerant. As shown in the diagram, the Web tier, Application tier, and Database tier are clustered, which means that if any nodes from these tiers go down, the system will still respond to user requests.

Security

The reference architecture places Firewall in front of the Hardware Load Balancer, which ensures that all the security threats are filtered. Depending upon the security needs, it is advisable to set up a firewall between each tier as well. So for example, the Web tier can access the Application tier, but the opposite can be prevented. Depending upon the project need, the architecture supports configuring SSL-based access.

The Deployment sizing approach

In the previous section, we learned about the Liferay Portal reference architecture. The reference architecture is generic in nature. It can be used as a reference to define an architecture that is more specific to a project. One of the important activities in defining a specific architecture is **sizing**. We need to be sure of the number of Liferay Portal application servers or web servers to meet performance expectations. In the beginning of the project when the system is yet to be developed, it is impossible to size the architecture with 100 percent accuracy. Hence, the idea is to size the architecture based on previous benchmarks, and then review the sizing during the load testing phase when the system is ready. Liferay Inc. publishes the performance benchmark for every major Liferay Portal release. It is a best practice to use this benchmark as a reference and size the deployment architecture of the solution. In this section, we will learn how to size the deployment architecture of the Liferay-Portal-based solution based on Liferay's performance benchmark whitepaper.

>  This section refers to the Liferay Portal 6.1 performance white paper published by Liferay Inc.. This whitepaper can be accessed through the following URL:
> `http://discover.liferay.com/LP=13/?i=Liferay_Portal_6.1`

The first step of the sizing activity is to capture some of the basic non-functional requirements. The following table provides a list of these questions. The answers to these questions will act as parameters for sizing calculations.

No.	The requirement question	Mandatory?	Details
1	How many concurrent users will log in at the same time?	Yes	Login is the most resource-consuming use case in Liferay Portal. It is very important to know the answer to this question.
2	What is the number of concurrent users accessing the Message Board functionality including login?	No	The Liferay performance benchmark report publishes the result of this scenario. If the project requirement matches the scenario, we can use this to size the deployment architecture more accurately.

No.	The requirement question	Mandatory?	Details
3	What is the number of concurrent users accessing the Blogging functionality including login?	No	If such a scenario is applicable to our requirement, we can derive a more accurate deployment architecture.
4	What is the number of concurrent users accessing the document management functionality including login?	No	Depending upon the project requirement if such a scenario exists, using this parameter we can size the deployment architecture more accurately.

Once we get the answers to these questions, the next step is to compare the answers with performance benchmark results from the white paper and derive the exact number of application servers we will need. The whitepaper establishes linear scalability based on various tests. Based on the report, we can establish the exact number of application servers that we will need to handle a specific number of concurrent users. Before we jump on to the calculation, let us summarize the performance benchmark report.

The reference hardware

In the performance benchmark test, Liferay Inc. used the following hardware configurations:

Server type	Configuration
Apache Web Server	1 x Intel Core 2 Duo E6405 2.13 GHz CPU, 2 MB L2 cache (2 cores in total)
	4 GB memory, 1 x 146 GB 7.2k RPM IDE
Liferay Portal Application Server	2 x Intel Core 2 Quad X5677 3.46 GHz CPU, 12 MB L2 cache (8 cores and 16 threads)
	16 GB memory, 2 x 146 GB 10k RPM SCSI
Database Server	2 x Intel Core 2 Quad X5677 3.46 GHz CPU, 12 MB L2 cache (8 cores and 16 threads)
	16 GB memory, 4 x 146 GB 15k RPM SCSI

The performance benchmark test summary

In the performance benchmark test, Liferay Inc. concluded the following:

No.	Scenario	Result summary
1	**Isolated logins**: During this test, a number of concurrent users tried to log in at the same time. Based on this scenario, the breaking point of the Liferay Portal application server was identified. In this scenario, no customizations were considered and the Liferay login scenario with out of the box home page was tested.	According to the results, one Liferay Portal application server was able to handle 27,000 concurrent logins at the same time. After , concurrent login requests if we increase the requests, the application starts becoming loaded and the response time increases.
2	**Login with Legacy Simulator**: In this scenario a two-second delay was included in one of the home page portlets. As we build our application on top of Liferay Portal and we normally have some additional processing time after login for custom home page portlets, a delay of two seconds was included to simulate this scenario. This is the realistic scenario for estimating possible concurrent logins by a server.	The results proved that the performance of the system degrades after 6,300 concurrent login requests. That means one application server should handle 6,300 concurrent login requests only. If expected concurrent users are more than 6,300 but less than 12,600 concurrent requests, one more application server should be added in the cluster.
3	**Message Board**: In this scenario, a number of concurrent users will log in and perform various transactions on the Message Board portlet.	It was proved that one application server was stable until 5,800 concurrent requests. After that, the system performance started to degrade. So in this scenario, one application server was able to handle 5,800 concurrent requests smoothly.
4	**Blogging**: In this scenario, a number of concurrent users performed blogging transactions, such as view blog list, view blog entry, post new blog, and so on.	The result proved that one application server was able to handle 6,000 concurrent requests smoothly.
5	**Document management**: In this scenario, a number of concurrent users accessed document management functionalities.	The results proved that the system was able to handle 5,400 concurrent requests smoothly with one application server.

An example of sizing calculations

We learned about the reference hardware and benchmark results. Now, let's size the deployment architecture for a sample project.

Sample performance requirements

The example Portal solution should be able to handle 15,000 concurrent requests. This is the only requirement that we received from the customer, and we need to size our initial deployment architecture based on that.

Sizing calculations

Login is the most resource-consuming operation in a Liferay-based portal. Also, the login use case takes care of authentication as well as rendering of the home page, which is displayed after authentication. We have not received any use case-specific performance needs. So for sizing, we can refer to the benchmark results of the Login with Legacy Simulator scenario. According to the results of this benchmark test, one Liferay Portal application server can handle 6,300 concurrent login requests. So to handle 15,000 concurrent login requests, we will need three Liferay Portal application servers. Generally, the load on the web server is less than 50 percent of application servers. Hence, we can derive the number of web servers as half of the application servers. So in our case, we will need two web servers (3 application servers/2). For the database server as per our reference architecture, it is recommended to have a master-slave database server. This calculation is valid for similar hardware configurations as it was used in the benchmark performance test. Hence, we need to use the same hardware configuration for the application server, web server, and database servers.

> This calculation is an initial sizing calculation. More accurate sizing calculations can be done only after the system is developed and load testing is performed.

The Documents and Media Library architecture

Documents and Media Library is one of the most important functionality of Liferay Portal. It allows users to manage documents, images, videos, and other types of documents. This functionality is designed in such a way that metadata is stored in the database, while actual files are stored on pluggable repository stores. Liferay Portal ships with various built-in repository stores. In this section, we will learn about these repository stores and the best practices associated with them.

File System and Advanced File System stores

Both File System store and Advance File System store are similar with some exceptions. Both of these store files on the filesystem. Advanced File System stores additionally distributes files in a multiple folder structure to eliminate limitations of the filesystem. The File System store is the default repository store used by Liferay Portal. Compared to other repository stores, both of these stores give better performance.

Liferay doesn't handle file locking when we use any of these two stores. Hence on production environments, they must be used with Storage Area Network (SAN) with file locking capabilities. Most of the SAN providers support file locking, but this has to be verified before using them.

To get best performance results, it is recommended to use an Advanced File System store with SAN. In our reference architecture, we have used the same approach for the Media Library repository. Liferay can be configured to use the Advanced File System store by using the following properties in `portal-ext.properties`:

```
dl.store.impl=com.liferay.portlet.documentlibrary.store.AdvancedFileSystemStore
dl.store.file.system.root=<Location of the SAN directory>
```

The Database store

This repository store simply stores files in the Liferay database. Concurrent access to files is automatically managed as files are stored in the database. From the performance point of view, this store will give bad results when compared to File System and Advanced File System stores. Also, if the Portal is expected to have heavy use of the Media Library functionality, then this repository store will also affect the overall performance of the Portal, as the load on the database will increase for file management. It is not recommended to use this store unless the use of the Media Library is limited. Liferay Portal can be configured to use the Database store by adding the following property in `portal-ext.properties`:

```
dl.store.impl=com.liferay.portlet.documentlibrary.store.DBStore
```

The JCR store

Java Content Repository (**JCR**) is the result of the standardization of content repositories used across content management systems. It follows the JSR-170 standard specification. Liferay Portal also provides the JCR store, which can be configured with the Media Library. The JCR store internally uses Apache Jackrabbit, which is an implementation of JSR-170. Apache Jackrabbit also, by default, stores files in a filesystem. It can be also configured to use the database for storing medial library files. For the production environment if we plan to use JCR, it must be configured to store files in the database. As on a filesystem, we can get file locking issues. The JCR store is a good option for the production environment when it is not possible to use the Advanced File System store with SAN. To configure Liferay to use the JCR store, we need to add the following properties to `portal-ext.properties`:

```
dl.store.impl=com.liferay.portlet.documentlibrary.store.JCRStore
```

The CMIS store

Content Management Interoperability Services (**CMIS**) is an open standard that defines services for controlling document management repositories. It was created to standardize content management services across multiple platforms. It is the latest standard used by most of the content management systems to make content management systems interoperable. It uses web services and RESTful services that any application can access. Liferay provides the CMIS store which can connect to any CMIS-compatible content repositories. The metadata of the Media Library content will be stored in Liferay, and the actual files will be stored in the external CMIS-compatible repository. This repository store can be used when we need to integrate Liferay Portal with external repositories. For example, Alfresco is one of the leading open source content management systems. If we have a requirement to integrate the Alfresco content repository with Liferay, we can use the CMIS store which will internally connect with Alfresco using CMIS services. To configure Liferay with the CMIS repository, we need to add the following properties to `portal-ext.properties`:

```
dl.store.impl=com.liferay.portlet.documentlibrary.store.CMISStore
dl.store.cmis.credentials.username=<User Name to be used for CMIS authentication>
dl.store.cmis.credentials.password=<Password to be used for CMIS authentication>
dl.store.cmis.repository.url=<URL of CMIS Repository>
dl.store.cmis.system.root.dir=Liferay Home
```

The S3 store

Nowadays, companies are moving their infrastructures to the cloud. It provides great benefit in procuring and managing hardware infrastructure. It also allows us to increase or decrease the infrastructure capacity quickly. One of the most popular cloud providers is Amazon AWS. Amazon offers a cloud-based storage service called **Amazon Simple Storage Service (Amazon S3)**. The Liferay Media Library can be configured to store Media Library files on Amazon S3. This is a good option when the production environment is deployed on the Amazon Cloud infrastructure. To configure Liferay to use Amazon S3 for the Media Library store, we need to add the following properties to `portal-ext.properties`:

```
dl.store.impl=com.liferay.portlet.documentlibrary.store.S3Store
dl.store.s3.access.key=<amazon s3 access key id>
dl.store.s3.secret.key=<amazon s3 encrypted secret access key>
dl.store.s3.bucket.name=<amazon s3's root folder name>
```

The database architecture

Liferay Portal requires storing its data on database systems. It is possible to store custom portlet data in a separate database. But for the core features of Liferay Portal, we need to connect Liferay with a database. In our reference architecture, we suggested using the MySQL cluster for this purpose. In this section, we will talk about various deployment strategies for the database server.

The read/write database

In case of transaction-centric applications, it is a good idea to separate read and write databases. In this situation, all write transactions will be executed on the write database and all read transactions will be executed on the read-only database. Using database replication mechanism, data from the write database is replicated to the read database. By using this mechanism, we can optimize the write database to perform extensive write transactions and the read database to perform extensive read transactions. Liferay Portal supports configuring read and write databases through `portal-ext.properties`. Here are some high-level steps to configure the read/write database through `portal-ext.properties`.

1. In `portal-ext.properties`, append the following value at the end of original values. This configuration change will load the following spring configuration file during startup and load the rest of the read/write database properties:

   ```
   spring.configs=<Existing config files>, META-INF/dynamic-data-source-spring.xml
   ```

2. Add the following properties to `portal-ext.properties` to configure the read database:

   ```
   jdbc.read.driverClassName=<Read Database Driver Class Name>
   jdbc.read.url=<Read Database JDBC URL>
   jdbc.read.username=<Read Database User Name>
   jdbc.read.password=<Read Database Password>
   ```

3. Add the following properties to `portal-ext.properties` to configure the write database:

   ```
   jdbc.write.driverClassName=<Read Database Driver Class Name>
   jdbc.write.url=<Read Database JDBC URL>
   jdbc.write.username=<Read Database User Name>
   jdbc.write.password=<Read Database Password>
   ```

> If data sources are configured through JNDI, we need to configure the `jdbc.read.jndi.name` and `jdbc.write.jndi.name` properties respectively for the read data source and the write data source.

Database sharding

Database sharding is the architectural solution to separate the data of same the tables in multiple database instances. Liferay supports this feature. Liferay Portal can be used to host multiple portals within the same portal server using Portal Instances (Companies). By default, Liferay Portal stores data of all the instances in the same database. If we are hosting multiple portals using portal instances, the same tables will have data from multiple instances. Gradually, tables will grow rapidly because of the data from multiple portals. At some point in time, this will affect the performance as tables grow rapidly, and for any request internally the system will need to scan the data of all instances. We can configure multiple database shards (separate databases), and we can provide how shards should be chosen. Depending on the shard selection algorithm, each portal instance will be mapped to a specific shard database. By using this architectural approach, data from multiple instances will be distributed in multiple databases. By default, Liferay supports configuring three shards. But we can add more shards by changing configuration files. We can enable database sharding by changing `portal-ext.properties`. Here are some high-level steps to configure database sharding:

1. Append the following property in `portal-ext.properties` to enable database sharding:

   ```
   spring.configs=<Existing config files>, META-INF/shard-data-source-spring.xml
   ```

2. Configure database shards by adding the following properties in `portal-ext.properties`:

```
#Shard 1
jdbc.default.driverClassName=<Database Driver Class Name for shard 1>
jdbc.default.url=<Database JDBC URL for shard 1>
jdbc.default.username=<Database User Name for shard 1>
jdbc.default.password=<Database Password for shard 1>
#Shard 2
jdbc.one.driverClassName=<Database Driver Class Name for shard 2>
jdbc.one.url=<Database JDBC URL for shard 2>
jdbc.one.username=<Database User Name for shard 2>
jdbc.one.password=<Database Password for shard 2>
#shard 3
jdbc.two.driverClassName=<Database Driver Class Name for shard 3>
jdbc.two.url=<Database JDBC URL for shard 3>
jdbc.two.username=<Database User Name for shard 3>
jdbc.two.password=<Database Password for shard 3>
```

> If we want to add more than three shards, we will need to provide our own `shard-data-source-spring.xml` with more than three shards, and we need to provide s similar configuration in `portal-ext.properties` for those additional shards.

By default, shards will be assigned to each portal instance based on the round ribbon algorithm. Liferay also supports the manual selection algorithm. This algorithm allows for the selecting of a specific shard through the control panel. To enable the manual shard selection algorithm, we need to add the following property in `portal-ext.properties`:

```
shard.selector=com.liferay.portal.dao.shard.ManualShardSelector
```

Static content delivery

In any dynamic web application, majority of the web requests are for static resources, such as JavaScript, CSS, images, or videos. The same rule also applies to Liferay-Portal-based solutions. Hence, it is very important from an architectural point of view how we serve these static resources. In a basic Liferay Portal setup, static resources are served from the Liferay Portal application server. In this section, we will learn about other options to serve static resources.

Content Delivery Network

Content Delivery Network (CDN) is a large network of servers deployed across the world to serve static resources. The same static resources are stored on multiple servers across the world. When these static resources are requested, they will be retrieved from a server nearby the location of user. This feature reduces response time drastically. Liferay Portal also supports integration with CDNs. In Liferay Portal, majority of the static resources are a part of themes. Liferay provides a way to rewrite URLs of static resources within themes to a URL of the same resource in CDN. By using this feature, we can also reduce the load on the Liferay Portal application server by reducing the number of requests. To configure Liferay with CDN, we need to perform the following steps:

1. Upload all the static resources from the theme into CDN. CDN providers provide the UI to do the same. This step requires referring to the CDN provider's documentation.

2. Add the following properties to the `portal-ext.properties` file:

   ```
   cdn.host.http=<CDN host name to server static resources from http request>
   cdn.host.https=<CDN host name to server static resources from https request>
   ```

This solution is highly recommended when the intended users are spread across the globe.

Content delivery through the web server

If we serve static resources directly from the web server, it can reduce the number of requests coming to the Liferay Portal application server. Also, static resources can be served faster from the web server than the application server. All portal requests pass through the web server. Hence, it is easy to filter static resource requests and serve them directly from the web server. To implement this option, we do not need to change any configuration on the Liferay Portal application. We need to copy all static resources from all the Liferay plugins to the web server public directory. We need to make changes in the web server configuration so that all the static resource requests are directly served from the web server public directory. In this approach, we need to ensure that we copy the static resources to the web server every time we deploy a new version. This option can be used along with CDN to serve static resources of portlets.

It is recommended to create an automated shell script to copy static resources from the Liferay Portal application server to the Apache web server as a part of the deployment process.

The caching architecture

Caching is a very important aspect for any system to achieve high performance. Liferay Portal provides integration with different caching frameworks. Liferay Portal, by default, caches entity records, content, and so on. In this section, we will learn about various caching options available with Liferay Portal.

Caching using Ehcache

Ehcache is a very powerful-distributed caching framework. Liferay Portal, by default, comes with the Ehcache integration. The default configuration uses a cache on local instances. This means that if we are using a clustered environment, each node will have its own cache. So in a clustered environment, it is required to replicate the cache across all the nodes. There are different options available to replicate a cache across multiple nodes. Here are the options available to replicate Ehcache across the cluster.

Ehcache replication using RMI

Ehcache framework supports cache replication using RMI. In this scenario, when the server starts up using IP multicast, each node in the cluster will connect with other nodes using RMI. All the cache updates are replicated to other nodes using RMI. It is a kind of point-to-point connection between all the nodes in the cluster. The following diagram explains how each node connects with the other to replicate the cache:

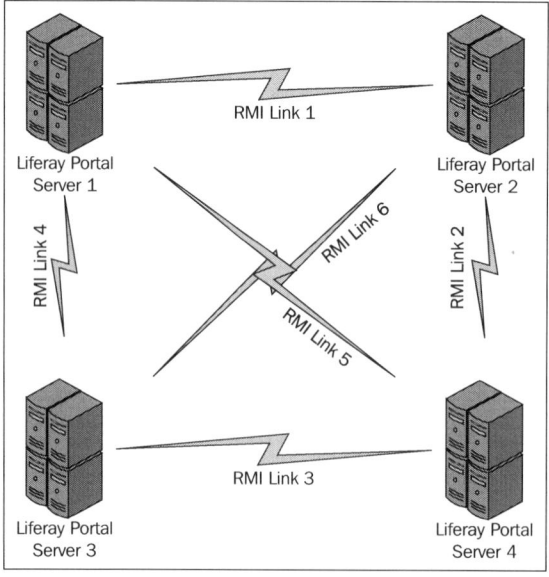

As shown in the preceding diagram, we have four Liferay Portal nodes in the cluster. Each node is connected with each other. So in total, it will create around twelve RMI links to replicate the cache across other nodes. This option uses a thread-per-cache replication algorithm. Hence, it creates a massive number of threads for replicating the cache over the cluster. Because of this algorithm, this option adds a lot of overhead and affects the overall performance of the system.

Ehcache replication using Cluster Link

This option is available for the enterprise version of Liferay Portal. In this approach, Liferay Portal creates a limited number of dispatcher threads that are responsible for replicate cache over the cluster. As in this approach all requests pass through a single place before they are actually distributed in the network, it gives a chance to remove unnecessary requests. For example, if the same cache object is changed by multiple nodes, instead of sending two requests to all the nodes to invalidate cache, only one request will be sent. This feature reduces network traffic. The following architectural diagram explains this feature in detail:

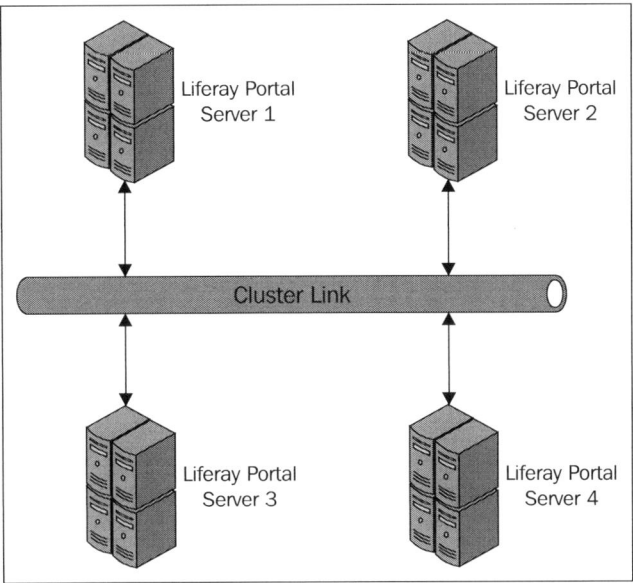

As shown in the preceding diagram, all four Liferay Portal nodes are connected to each other using Cluster Link. Internally, this feature uses UDP multicast to establish a connection with cluster nodes. A small group of threads is created to distribute cache update events to all the connected nodes. It is recommended to use this option for Ehcache replication.

Caching using Terracotta

In the previous section, we talked about Liferay Ehcache integration. In order to use Ehcache in a distributed environment, we need to replicate the cache across the cluster. Another approach is to use the centralized caching server. All nodes connect to the centralized cache server and store/retrieve cached objects. In this approach, we do not need to worry about cache replication. Terracotta is one of the leading products which provides this solution. Liferay Portal supports integration with Terracotta. If a portal is intended to have a large amount of cache objects and a large number of cache changes, it is recommended to go with this approach. Terracotta also provides solutions for storing web sessions and quartz jobs. By using Terracotta, we can even prevent session replication and replication of quartz job data. The following diagram explains how Terracotta fits into the Liferay Portal architecture:

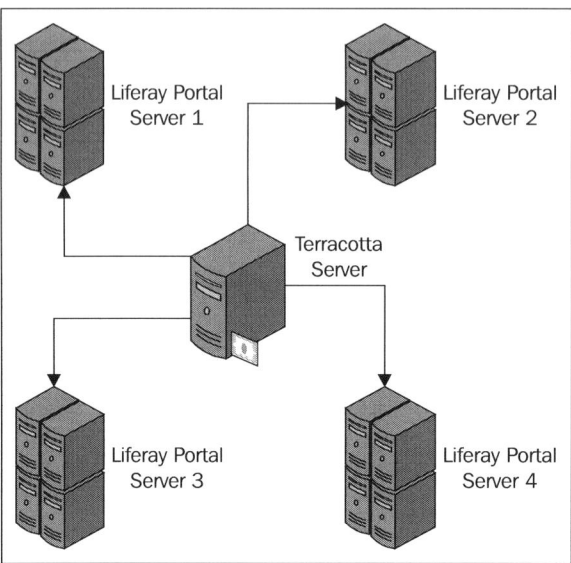

As shown in the preceding diagram when we use Terracotta, we will not need any communication between individual Liferay Portal application nodes. Each node will directly communicate with Terracotta and store/retrieve cached objects, sessions, and quartz data. It is recommended to use this architectural approach if the portal is going to have huge cache objects. This approach gives the best performance by omitting replication overhead.

Web resource caching using Varnish

We have talked about the caching of objects at the Application tier. But in many situations, it is even possible to cache whole web pages and deliver them directly from the cache. This option can be used for content that doesn't change frequently. This approach can reduce the load on the web server, application server, and database server drastically, and also improve the overall response time. Such caching tools are also called **web application accelerators**. Varnish is one of the popular open source web application accelerators.

The following architectural diagram explains where Varnish can fit in our reference architecture:

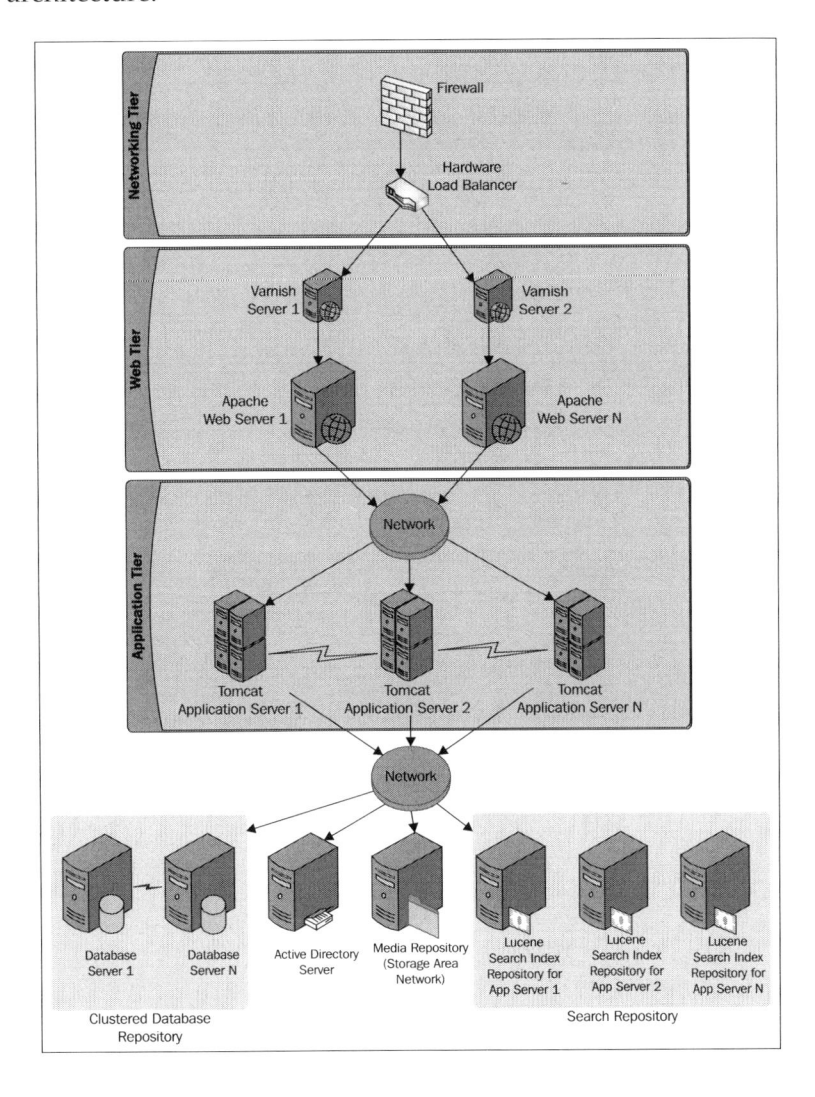

Architectural Best Practices

As shown in the preceding diagram, the Varnish server runs in front of web servers. The Hardware load balancer will sent all the requests to the Varnish server. Based on the configuration, the Varnish server will decide if the request should be served from the cache or should be send to the web server. It provides a way to clear the cache as well. Depending upon the hardware configuration of the web server, it is also possible to run the Varnish server on the web server itself. This architectural option can be used with many portals which serves kind of static contents. Some of the examples include news portals and product catalogue portals.

> For more information about Varnish please refer to the following URL:
> `https://www.varnish-cache.org/`

The search architecture

Search is an inescapable feature in every portal application. Liferay Portal also provides search functionality out of the box. Liferay Portal includes the search framework which can be integrated with external search engines. In this section, we will look at various search integration options available with Liferay Portal.

Apache Lucene

Liferay Portal, by default, uses the embedded Apache Lucene search engine. Apache Lucene is the leading open source search engine available in the market. By default, Liferay Portal's search API connects with the local embedded Lucene search engine. It stores search indexes on the local filesystem. When we use Lucene in a clustered environment, we need to make sure the indexes are replicated across the cluster. There are different approaches to make sure the same search indexes are available to all Liferay Portal nodes.

Index storage on SAN

One of the options is to configure Lucene to store indexes on a centralized network location. Hence, all the Liferay Portal nodes will refer to the same version of indexes. Liferay provides a way to configure indexes on a particular location. This approach is recommended only if we have SAN installed, and the SAN provider handles file locking issues. As indexes are accessed and changed too often, if SAN is not able to handle file locking issues, we will end up having problems with the search functionality. This option gives the best performance. To configure the location of the index directory, we need to add the following property in `portal-ext.properties`:

```
lucene.dir=<SAN lucene index location>
```

Lucene Index replication using Cluster Link

We have learned about the Cluster Link feature of Liferay Portal which replicates Ehcache. Cluster Link also replicates Lucene indexes across the Liferay Portal nodes. Cluster Link connects to all the Liferay Portal nodes using UDP multicast. When Cluster Link is enabled, the Liferay search engine API raises an event on Cluster Link to replicate specific index changes across the cluster. The Cluster Link dispatcher threads distribute index changes to other nodes. This is a very powerful feature. This feature doesn't require specialized hardware. But it adds overhead on the network and the Liferay Portal server. This option is recommended if we cannot go with centralized index storage on SAN.

Apache Solr

Apache Solr is one of the powerful open source search engines. It is based on the Apache Lucene search engine. In simple words, it wraps the Lucene search engine and provides access to Lucene search engine APIs through web services. Unlike Lucene, Solr runs as a separate web application. Liferay provides integration with Apache Solr as well. To integrate Apache Solr with Liferay, we need to install the Solr web plugin. We can configure the URL of the Solr server by modifying the configuration of the Solr web plugin. It is recommended to use Solr with Liferay Portal when the Portal is expected to write a large amount of data in search indexes. In such situations, Apache Lucene will add a lot of overhead due to index replication over the cluster. As Apache Solr runs as a separate web application, it makes the Portal architecture more scalable. The following diagram explains the basic Liferay-Solr integration:

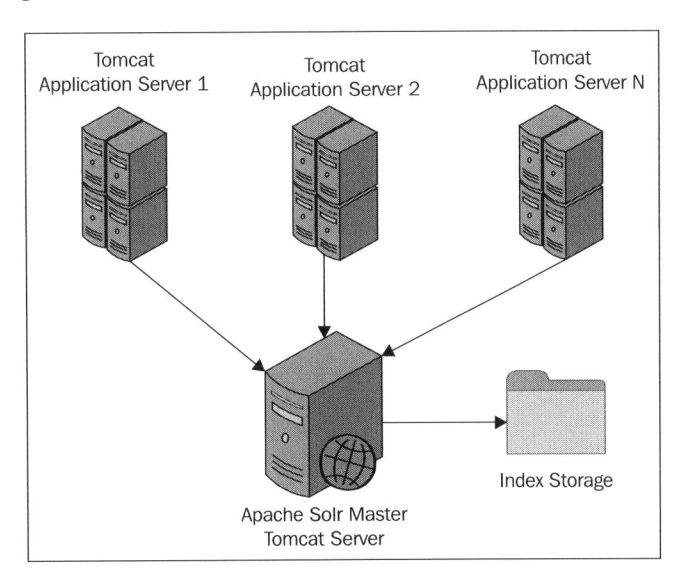

Architectural Best Practices

As shown in the preceding diagram, Apache Solr is installed on a separate server. The Apache Solr server internally stores indexes on the filesystem. All Liferay Portal servers are connected with the Apache Solr server. Every search request and index write request will be sent to the Apache Solr server.

In the preceding architecture, we are using a single Solr server for both read and write operations. Internally, the Solr server performs concurrent read and write operations on the same index storage. If the Portal application is expected to perform heavy write and search operations on the Solr server, this architecture as explained earlier will not give good performance. In such situations, it is recommended to use the master-slave Solr setup. In this approach, one master and many slave Solr servers are configured to work together. The master server will handle all the write operations and the slave servers will handle all read and search operations. Here is the diagram explaining the master-slave Solr setup:

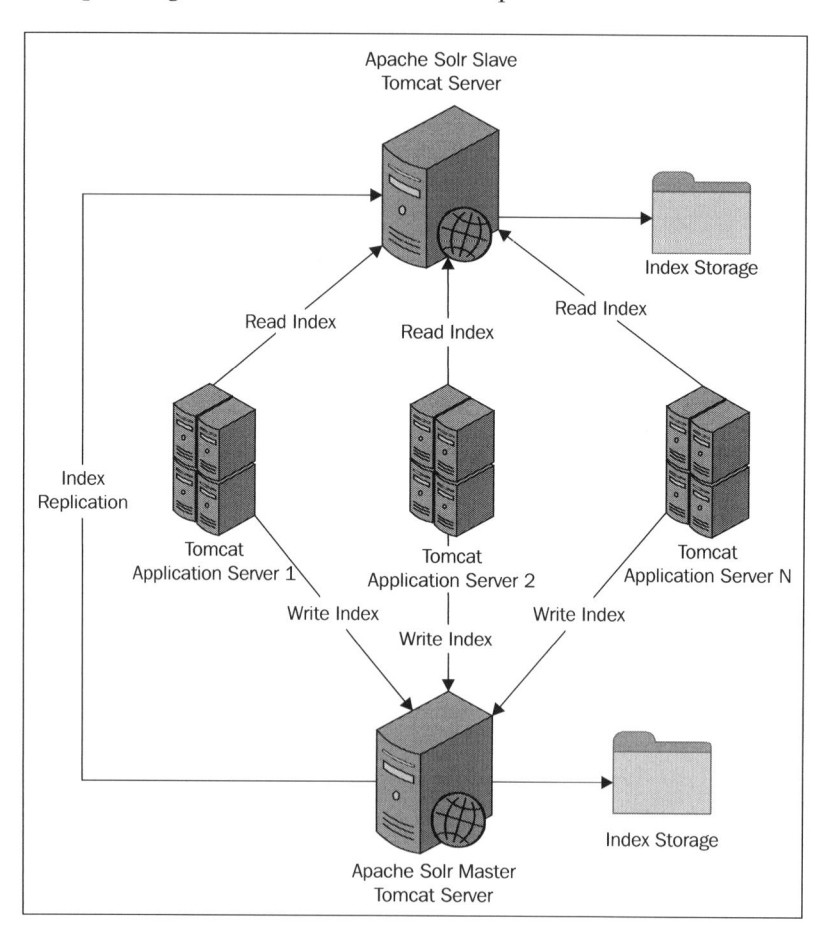

As shown in the preceding diagram, we have one Solr master server and one Solr slave server. The Solr master server is configured such that it automatically replicates indexes to the slave server. Each Liferay Portal application server will be connected to both master and slave servers. The Liferay Solr web plugin provides a way to configure separate Solr servers for read and write operations. To scale the search functionality further, we can also configure separate slave servers for each Liferay portal node. This will reduce the load on the slave server by limiting search requests.

Summary

We have covered most of the important architectural aspects that we should consider while designing a Liferay-based portal. We learned about the reference architecture of Liferay-Portal-based solutions and the sizing approach. We also learned about various architectural options for managing the Document and Medial library, caching, and static content delivery. We also talked about caching options available to boost performance. In the last section, we learned various architectural options available for the search functionality.

Now let's get ready to learn about load balancing and clustering in detail.

Load Balancing and Clustering Best Practices

In the previous chapter, we learned the reference architecture and architectural best practices of Liferay-Portal-based solutions. One of the key architectural concepts which we learned in the previous chapter is **load balancing** and **clustering**. We learned how horizontal scaling can fulfill performance and scalability needs. In this chapter, we will learn how to configure the software load balancer and cluster for Liferay-Portal-based solutions. We will also learn the best practices associated with each configuration step. We will cover the following topics in this chapter:

- Basics of load balancing and clustering with Liferay
- Load balancer configuration
    - Apache Web Server configuration
    - Application Server configuration
- Clustering configuration
- Ehcache configuration
- Media Library configuration
- Search configuration
- Quartz job configuration

Let's gear up to start with the basics of load balancing and clustering with Liferay.

The basics of load balancing and clustering with Liferay

Load balancing is a technique to distribute load on multiple systems. In the previous chapter, we talked about the reference architecture of Liferay-Portal-based solutions. In our reference architecture, we referred to two levels of load balancing. The first level of load balancing is done by the hardware load balancer. The hardware load balancer distributes load among Apache Web Servers. As hardware load balancing is very specific to the load balancer appliance, we will not cover it in this book. The second level of load balancing is done by Apache web servers. Each Apache web server performs the role of software load balancer and distributes load among Liferay Portal application servers. In this chapter, we will focus on Apache Web Server based software load balancing.

To learn best practices associated with load balancing and clustering of Liferay-Portal-based solutions, we need to know how to configure the load balancer and cluster. In the next few sections, we will learn how to configure the cluster of Liferay Portal servers, which is similar to our reference architecture.

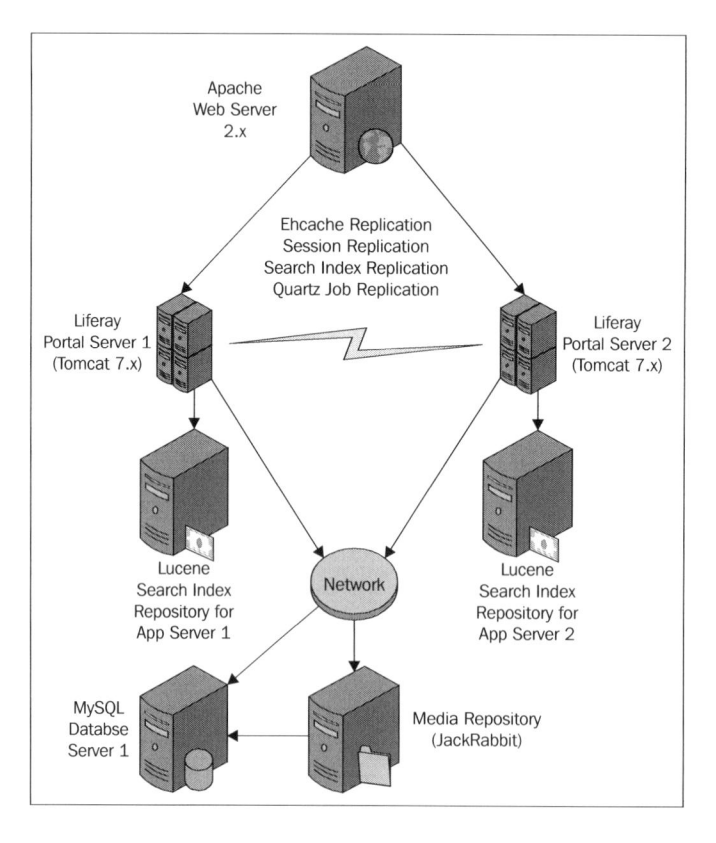

As shown in the preceding diagram, we will configure the cluster of two Liferay Portal application servers. We will need the following software components to set up the clustered environment:

- Liferay Portal Community Edition 6.1 GA2
- Apache Web Server 2.X
- MySQL Community Server 5.5.29

> It is not mandatory to use the exact versions as mentioned, but the exercises within this chapter are verified on the versions listed.

To configure the Liferay Portal cluster as shown in the preceding architecture diagram, we will need four servers to set up the Apache Web Server, MySQL Database server, and two Liferay Portal application servers. It is assumed that Apache Web Server and MySQL Community Server are already installed and running. Once these prerequisites are addressed, we will need to perform the following high-level steps to configure the clustered environment:

- Setting up Liferay Portal Server nodes
- Software load balancer configuration using Apache Web Server
- Liferay Portal session replication configuration
- Liferay Portal Media Library configuration
- Liferay Portal Ehcache configuration
- Liferay Portal search configuration
- Liferay Portal quartz scheduler configuration

So let's start with Liferay Portal cluster configuration steps.

Setting up Liferay Portal nodes

As shown in the architecture diagram, we need to configure two Liferay Portal server nodes. Throughout the book, we will refer to both Liferay Portal servers as `liferay-node-01` and `liferay-node-02` respectively. Let's do that by following the ensuing steps:

1. On `liferay-node-01`, create a directory named `node-01` in the root directory, and then extract the Liferay Portal 6.1 GA2 bundle in it. Similarly on `liferay-node-02`, create a directory name, `node-02`, and extract the Liferay Portal bundle in it.

> We created node-01 and node-02 directories for easy reference to the Liferay installation directory throughout the book. It may not be required on production setup. Throughout the book we will refer to the node-01 directory for Liferay Portal installation on the liferay-node-01 server and the node-02 directory for Liferay Portal installation on the liferay-node-02 server.

2. Create a new database schema in the MySQL Database server using the following command:

   ```
   create database lportal character set utf8;
   ```

3. Now create the portal-ext.properties file in the node-01\liferay-portal-6.1.1-ce-ga2& node-02\liferay-portal-6.1.1-ce-ga2 directory with the following content:

   ```
   jdbc.default.driverClassName=com.mysql.jdbc.Driver
   jdbc.default.url=jdbc:mysql://<MySQL Database Server IP>/lportal?useUnicode=true&characterEncoding=UTF-8&useFastDateParsing=false
   jdbc.default.username=<MySQL Database User Name>
   jdbc.default.password=<MySQL Password>
   ```

> Make sure you provide the correct IP, username, and password of the MySQL server with which the lportal database is accessible.

We just installed the Liferay Portal server on both the Liferay portal nodes. We created a database in the MySQL server and provided database configuration on both the Liferay Portal nodes using the portal-ext.properties file.

> In the book, we are implementing horizontal scaling as both the Liferay Portal nodes are on separate servers. But suppose we want to implement vertical scaling by installing both the Liferay Portal nodes on the same server, we will need to make sure that unique ports are used for both the Liferay Portal nodes. For the Liferay Portal Tomcat bundle, ports can be configured in server.xml.

Software load balancer configuration using the Apache Web Server

Now, both the Liferay Portal server nodes are ready. As a next step, we need to configure the Apache Web Server to connect with both the Liferay Portal nodes and also distribute the load on both the Liferay Portal nodes. The Apache Web Server provides many options to connect with the Liferay Portal Tomcat server. But there are three options which are more popular. Let's understand these options and the scenarios in which they are best suitable.

Load balancer configuration using mod_jk

This option allows us to configure the load balancer using the mod_jk module of the Apache Web server. Internally, the mod_jk module connects with the Liferay Portal Tomcat server using the AJP protocol. Using this option, the Apache Web Server distributes all requests on the AJP port of Liferay Portal Tomcat servers. Let's learn how to configure the software load balancer using this option.

1. Download and copy the mod_jk module in the <APACHE_HOME>/modules directory.

   > The mod_jk connector is available for download from the following URL:
   > http://tomcat.apache.org/download-connectors.cgi

2. Create a new file called mod_jk.conf in the <APACHE_HOME>/conf directory, and add the following configuration into it:

   ```
   LoadModule      jk_module  modules/mod_jk.so
   JkWorkersFile   /etc/httpd/conf/workers.properties
   JkShmFile       /var/log/httpd/mod_jk.shm
   JkLogFile       /var/log/httpd/mod_jk.log
   JkLogLevel      info
   JkLogStampFormat "[%a %b %d %H:%M:%S %Y] "
   JkMount /* loadbalancer
   ```

   > In the preceding configuration, please make the changes to the file paths according to your installation folder structure.

3. Now edit the `httpd.conf` file located in the `<APACHE_HOME>/conf` directory, and add the following line at the bottom:

   ```
   Includemod_jk.conf
   ```

4. Add a new file called `worker.properties` in the `<APACHE_HOME>/conf` directory, and add the following lines into it:

   ```
   #Name of the load balancer workers
   worker.list=loadbalancer
   #Worker configuration for liferay-node-01
   #AJP Connector port of node-01 on liferay-node-01 server
   worker.node-01.port=8009
   worker.node-01.host=<IP of liferay-node-01 server>
   worker.node-01.type=ajp13
   #Factor which decides the load sharing by this worker in the cluster
   worker.node-01.lbfactor=1
   #Worker configuration for liferay-node-02
   worker.node-02.port=8009
   worker.node-02.host=<IP of liferay-node-02 server>
   worker.node-02.type=ajp13
   worker.node-02.lbfactor=1
   #load balancer configuration properties
   worker.loadbalancer.type=lb
   #list of worker nodes that are part of the cluster
   worker.loadbalancer.balance_workers=node-01,node-02
   worker.loadbalancer.sticky_session=1
   worker.loadbalancer.method=B
   ```

5. Now edit the `server.xml` file of `liferay-node-01` located in `node-01\liferay-portal-6.1.1-ce-ga2\tomcat-7.0.27\conf`, and add the `jvmRoute` attribute to the `<Engine>` tag as given here:

   ```
   <Engine defaultHost="localhost" name="Catalina" jvmRoute="node-01">
   ```

6. Similarly, add the `jvmRoute` parameter in `server.xml` of `liferay-node-02`. Here the value of `jvmRoute` will be `node-02`.

7. We are ready to test our configuration. Restart both the Liferay Portal nodes and the Apache Web Server to test the configuration. We can access Liferay Portal directly by using the `http://<Apache Web Server IP>` URL.

To connect the Apache Web Server with the Liferay Portal Tomcat server, we installed the `mod_jk` module in the Apache Web Server. We then configured the Apache Web Server to load the `mod_jk` module and provided the `mod_jk` configuration parameters. We defined the logfile and shared memory file locations and logfile formats for the `mod_jk` module. The most important configuration is to add worker nodes on which we want to distribute the load. We defined this by providing the `worker` configuration file. In the `worker` configuration file, we defined two Liferay Portal nodes. We then configured the load balancer and added Liferay Portal nodes to it. We configured the load balancer method to **Busyness** (**B**) which means, the load balancer will distribute the requests depending upon the load on Liferay Portal Tomcat servers. Other possible load balancer methods include **By Requests** (distributes the load based on the number of requests and load factor of the worker) and **By Traffic** (distributes load based on the traffic in bytes and load factor). Finally, we enabled session stickiness. Session stickiness is used to distribute all the requests for a specific session to a specific Liferay Portal Server node. Only in case of failure of the specific node, subsequent requests will be served by the other node. It is very important to use the sticky session feature to save resources. In order to make sure the sticky session functionality works fine, we configured `jvmRoute` in both the Tomcat nodes with unique values. The Apache Web Server appends `jvmRoute` in the session ID and based on the `jvmRoute` value, the Apache Web Server can ensure sending requests to the right Liferay Portal Tomcat node.

Load balancer configuration using mod_proxy_ajp

Another way to configure the software load balancer using Apache Web Server is through the `mod_proxy_ajp` and `mod_proxy_balancer` modules. This is a newer approach introduced in Apache Web Server 2.2. It uses the `mod_proxy` module and connects the Liferay Portal server using the AJP protocol. Let's understand how to configure the software load balancer using this option.

1. Create a new file called `mod_proxy_ajp.conf` in the `<APACHE_HOME>/conf` directory, and add the following content:

   ```
   LoadModuleproxy_modulemodules/mod_proxy.so
   LoadModule proxy_ajp_module modules/mod_proxy_ajp.so
   LoadModule proxy_balancer_module /modules/mod_proxy_balancer.so
   ```

   > If you are using an existing Apache Web Server, before adding these lines, make sure these modules are not enabled already in the Apache Web Server configuration (`<APACHE_HOME>/conf/httpd.conf` and all the included files).

Load Balancing and Clustering Best Practices

2. In the same file, add the following configuration settings:

   ```
   <VirtualHost *:80>
     ServerName localhost.localdomain
     ErrorLog /var/log/apache2/ajp.error.log
     CustomLog /var/log/apache2/ajp.log combined

     <Proxy *>
       AddDefaultCharSet Off
       Order deny,allow
       Allow from all
     </Proxy>
     ProxyPass / balancer://ajpCluster/ stickysession=JSESSIONID
     ProxyPassReverse / balancer://ajpCluster/ stickysession=JSESSIONID
     <Proxy balancer://ajpCluster>
       BalancerMember ajp://<IP of liferay-node-01>:8009 route=node-01
       BalancerMember ajp:// <IP of liferay-node-02>:8009 route=node-02
       ProxySet lbmethod=byrequests
     </Proxy>
   </VirtualHost>
   ```

3. Now edit the `httpd.conf` file located in the `<APACHE_HOME>/conf` directory, and add the following lines at the bottom:

   ```
   Include mod_proxy_ajp.conf
   ```

4. Now, edit the `server.xml` file of `liferay-node-01` located in `node-01\liferay-portal-6.1.1-ce-ga2\ tomcat-7.0.27\conf`, and add the `jvmRoute` attribute to the `<Engine>` tag as shown here:

   ```
   <Engine defaultHost="localhost" name="Catalina" jvmRoute="node-01">
   ```

5. Similarly, add the `jvmRoute` parameter in `server.xml` of `liferay-node-02`. Here the value of `jvmRoute` will be `node-02`.

6. Now restart both the Liferay Portal Servers and the Apache Web server, and test the configuration using the `http://<Apache Web Server IP>` URL.

This approach requires the `mod_proxy`, `mod_proxy_ajp` and `mod_proxy_balancer` modules. These modules, by default, ship with the Apache Web Server binary. We enabled them by using the `LoadModule` command. We then configured the virtual host for our local instance. In the virtual host configuration, we provided the locations of the logfiles. We added the load balancer using the `<Proxy balancer>` tag. Again in the load balancer configuration, we provided the hostname and port of both the Liferay Portal Servers. We also provided the `jvmRoute` value using the `route` parameter. This parameter must match with `jvmRoute` configured in steps 4 and 5. We also configured the load balancing method to **By Requests** (`byrequests`). This load balancing method distributes the load on both the Liferay Portal servers in a round robin manner. We also configured the virtual host to route all the requests to the load balancer using the `mod_proxy` configuration. We configured to use session stickiness through the `mod_proxy` configuration.

Load balancer configuration using mod_proxy_http

This method is very similar to `mod_proxy_ajp`. The only difference here is the load balancer configuration. Here the Apache Web Server and the Liferay Portal Tomcat server will connect using the HTTP or HTTPS protocol. So let's configure the load balancer using this option.

1. Similar to previous options, we need to load the necessary modules. Create a new file called `mod_proxy_http.conf` in the `<APACHE_HOME>/conf` directory and add the following content:

   ```
   LoadModuleproxy_modulemodules/mod_proxy.so
   LoadModule proxy_http_module modules/mod_proxy_http.so
   LoadModule proxy_balancer_module /modules/mod_proxy_balancer.so
   ```

   > If you are using an existing Apache Web Server, before adding these lines, make sure these modules are not already enabled in the Apache Web Server configuration.

2. In the same file, add the following configuration settings:

```
<VirtualHost *:80>
  ServerName localhost.localdomain
  ErrorLog /var/log/apache2/http.error.log
  CustomLog /var/log/apache2/http.log combined

  <Proxy *>
    AddDefaultCharSet Off
    Order deny,allow
    Allow from all
  </Proxy>
  ProxyPass / balancer://httpCluster/ stickysession=JSESSIONID
  ProxyPassReverse / balancer://httpCluster/ stickysession=JSESSIONID
  <Proxy balancer://httpCluster>
    BalancerMember http:// <IP of liferay-node-01>:8080 route=node-01
    BalancerMember http:// <IP of liferay-node-02>:8080 route=node-02
    ProxySet lbmethod=byrequests
  </Proxy>
</VirtualHost>
```

3. Now edit the `httpd.conf` file located in the `<APACHE_HOME>/conf` directory and add the following line at the bottom:

   ```
   Include mod_proxy_http.conf
   ```

4. Now edit the `server.xml` file of `liferay-node-01` located in `node-01\liferay-portal-6.1.1-ce-ga2\ tomcat-7.0.27\conf`, and add the `jvmRoute` attribute to the `<Engine>` tag as follows:

   ```
   <Engine defaultHost="localhost" name="Catalina" jvmRoute="node-01">
   ```

5. Similarly, add the `jvmRoute` parameter in `server.xml` of `liferay-node-02`. Here the value of `jvmRoute` will be `node-02`.

6. Now restart both the Liferay Portal Servers and the Apache Web server and test the configuration using the `http://<IP of Apache Web Server>` URL.

These steps are very similar to the previous option. The only difference is that we are using the HTTP protocol. This connector allows us to establish an encrypted connection between the web server and the Liferay Portal application server using the HTTPS protocol.

Load balancing best practices

We have learned three different methods of configuring the software load balancer using the Apache Web Server. Now let's learn some of the best practices associated with these options:

- The software load balancer configuration using `mod_jk` is most recommended because `mod_jk` is a reliable and error free module compared to other options. From the performance point of view it gives the best performance. The `mod_proxy_ajp` module is similar to `mod_jk` but it is relatively new. If there is a need to use a secured connection between the Apache Web Server and Liferay Portal Tomcat server, we can consider using the `mod_proxy_http` module. It provides easy configuration to implement this scenario.
- We learned that the Liferay Portal Tomcat server and the Apache Web Server either connect using the AJP connector or the HTTP connector. None of the connectors use both the connectors at the same time. The Liferay Portal Tomcat server, by default, enables both the connectors. It is a best practice to disable the connector which we are not using. This can save resources on the Liferay Portal application server. We can disable any of the connectors by commenting the respective `<Connector>` tag from the `server.xml` file of the Liferay Portal Tomcat server.
- It is advisable to select the load balancer method carefully. Depending upon the nature of the application, the right load balancer method should be chosen. If we are using the `mod_jk` connector, it is recommended to use the **Busyness** load balancer method. This will help in distributing requests on Liferay Portal servers with respect to their current load.

Liferay Portal cluster configuration

In the previous section, we learned about the software load balancer configuration using the Apache Web Server. In this section, we extend the setup by configuring the cluster between Liferay Portal Server nodes. To set up a cluster of Liferay Portal Server nodes, we need to ensure all shared resources are either centralized or replicated. The following list highlights the resources that need to be handled for cluster setup:

- **Liferay Portal web sessions**: For every user conversation, a web session object is created and managed by the Liferay Portal application server. A web session object stores important data related to a specific user conversation. In a clustered environment, it is possible that subsequent user requests are served by different Liferay Portal nodes. So, it is very important to make sure that the same session object is available on all clustered nodes.

- **Cache replication**: Liferay Portal, by default, uses the Ehcache caching framework for caching persistence and service layer resources. It is very important to invalidate or replicate caches across the cluster to avoid stale cache issues.

- **Media Library**: Media Library is one of the key features of Liferay. It is used to store documents, videos, images, and so on. Liferay stores the metadata of the Media Library content in the Liferay database, but the actual resources are stored using various repository stores. So, we need to ensure that the Media Library content is stored at a centralized place.

- **Search indexes**: Liferay provides a powerful built-in search feature. The default installation uses the Lucene search engine to provide search capability. The Lucene search engine stores the index on the filesystem. It is very important to ensure that search indexes are either centralized or replicated across all the nodes.

- **Quartz jobs**: There are various features in Liferay which internally use scheduled jobs. In a clustered environment, it is very important to ensure that all the nodes are aware about running scheduler jobs.

In this section, we will learn how to configure these resources to work in a clustered environment. We will also learn about the best practices associated with each option.

Session replication configuration

Session replication is a technique to replicate the session information across all the nodes. With the help of session replication, we can ensure automatic recovery after the failover of any node. In our load balancer configuration, we configured session stickiness which ensures all requests related to the same user session are served through a specific node. Now suppose that node goes down; in this case, the load balancer sends subsequent requests to another node in the cluster. If the new node does not have the session information of the same user, it considers it as a new session and in this situation the user will be logged out of the system. With the help of session replication, we can avoid this situation and ensure transparent switching between nodes.

Let's learn how to configure session replication.

1. Stop the Liferay Portal nodes if they are running.
2. Edit the `server.xml` file of `liferay-node-01` located in `node-01\liferay-portal-6.1.1-ce-ga2\ tomcat-7.0.27\conf`, and add the following configuration inside the `<Engine>` tag:

    ```
    <Cluster className="org.apache.catalina.ha.tcp.SimpleTcpCluster"
    channelSendOptions="6">
    ```

```xml
<Manager className="org.apache.catalina.ha.session.DeltaManager"
expireSessionsOnShutdown="false"
notifyListenersOnReplication="true"/>
<Channel className="org.apache.catalina.tribes.group.GroupChannel">
<Membership className="org.apache.catalina.tribes.membership.McastService"
address="228.0.0.4"
port="45564"
frequency="500"
dropTime="3000"/>
<Receiver className="org.apache.catalina.tribes.transport.nio.NioReceiver"
address="auto"
port="5000"
selectorTimeout="100"
maxThreads="6"/>

<Sender className="org.apache.catalina.tribes.transport.ReplicationTransmitter">
<Transport className="org.apache.catalina.tribes.transport.nio.PooledParallelSender"/>
</Sender>
<Interceptor className="org.apache.catalina.tribes.group.interceptors.TcpFailureDetector"/>
<Interceptor className="org.apache.catalina.tribes.group.interceptors.MessageDispatch15Interceptor"/>
<Interceptor className="org.apache.catalina.tribes.group.interceptors.ThroughputInterceptor"/>
</Channel>
<Valve className="org.apache.catalina.ha.tcp.ReplicationValve"
              filter=".*\.gif;.*\.js;.*\.jpg;.*\.png;.*\.htm;.*\.html;.*\.css;.*\.txt;"/>
<Valve className="org.apache.catalina.ha.session.JvmRouteBinderValve"/>

<ClusterListener className="org.apache.catalina.ha.session.JvmRouteSessionIDBinderListener"/>
<ClusterListener className="org.apache.catalina.ha.session.ClusterSessionListener"/>
</Cluster>
```

3. Edit the `web.xml` file of `liferay-node-01` located in `node-01\liferay-portal-6.1.1-ce-ga2\ tomcat-7.0.27\webapps\ROOT\WEB-INF` and at the bottom of the file before the `</web-app>` tag, add the following content:
   `<distributable/>`

4. Now repeat steps 2 and 3 on `liferay-node-02`.

5. Restart both the Liferay Portal nodes.

With this configuration, changes in session replication between both the Liferay Portal servers is set up. The Tomcat server provides a simple TCP cluster which connects multiple Tomcat servers using the TCP protocol. In our configuration, we used `DeltaManager` which identifies session changes and transfers these changes to other nodes in the cluster. We have used IP multicast to connect both the Tomcat servers. Once both the nodes connect with each other, they establish a set of sender and receiver socket channels. The session replication data is transferred using these channels. We have also configured various interceptors to intercept data transfer. The replication manager checks the session data after every request and accordingly transfers the changed session data to other nodes. For some kinds of requests, it is sure that the session data is not going to change; for example, requests for static resources like images, videos, and so on. So, it is unnecessary to check the session data after such requests. We configured a filter for all such resources in the replication valve configuration. The Application Server does not replicate sessions of any application unless the application is enabled for session replication. So, we enabled session replication for the Liferay Portal application by adding the `<distributable>` tag in `web.xml`.

Session replication is not a mandatory requirement for cluster configuration. Session replication consumes lots of server and network resources. So if there is not a real need to handle transparent failover, it is advisable to avoid session replication.

Cache replication

Caching is a very important technique to boost the performance of the system. Liferay Portal, by default, caches resources of the persistence layer and the service layer. By default, Liferay Portal uses the Ehcache framework for caching, and it caches resources in memory and the filesystem. In the clustered environment, each Liferay Portal node will have its own copy of the cache. It is very important to invalidate or replicate the cache on all the Liferay Portal nodes if the cache is invalidated or updated on any of the nodes. To implement this we need to replicate the cache. In this section, we will learn multiple options to replicate Ehcache across the cluster.

Ehcache replication using RMI

The Ehcache framework provides **RMI (Remote Method Invocation)** based cache replication across the cluster. It is the default implementation for replication. The RMI-based replication works on the TCP protocol. Cached resources are transferred using the serialization and deserialization mechanism of Java. RMI is a point-to-point protocol and hence, it generates a lot of network traffic between clustered nodes. Each node will connect to other nodes in the cluster and send cache replication messages. Liferay provides Ehcache replication configuration files in the bundle. We can re-use them to set up Ehcache replication using RMI. Let's learn how to configure Ehcache replication using RMI for our cluster.

1. Stop both the Liferay Portal nodes if they are running.

2. Add the following properties to the `portal-ext.properties` file of both the Liferay Portal nodes:

   ```
   net.sf.ehcache.configurationResourceName=/ehcache/hibernate-clustered.xml
   net.sf.ehcache.configurationResourceName.peerProviderProperties=peerDiscovery=automatic,multicastGroupAddress=${multicast.group.address["hibernate"]},multicastGroupPort=${multicast.group.port["hibernate"]},timeToLive=1
   ehcache.multi.vm.config.location=/ehcache/liferay-multi-vm-clustered.xml
   ehcache.multi.vm.config.location.peerProviderProperties=peerDiscovery=automatic,multicastGroupAddress=${multicast.group.address["multi-vm"]},multicastGroupPort=${multicast.group.port["multi-vm"]},timeToLive=1
   multicast.group.address["hibernate"]=233.0.0.4
   multicast.group.port["hibernate"]=23304
   multicast.group.address["multi-vm"]=233.0.0.5
   multicast.group.port["multi-vm"]=23305
   ```

3. Now restart both the Liferay Portal nodes.

Liferay Portal uses two separate Ehcache configurations for the hibernate cache and the Liferay service layer cache. Liferay ships with two different sets of configuration files for each hibernate and service layer cache. By default, it uses the non-replicated version of the cache file. Using the `portal-ext.properties` file, we can tell Liferay to use the replicated cache configuration file. In the preceding steps, we configured the replicated version of cache files for both the hibernate and service layer cache using the `net.sf.ehcache.configurationResourceName` and `ehcache.multi.vm.config.location` properties. Replicated Ehcache configuration files internally use IP multicast to establish the RMI connection between each Liferay node. We configured IP multicast and ports for establishing connections.

Ehcache configuration using JGroups

Another option to replicate Ehcache is using JGroups. JGroups is a powerful framework used for multicast communication. The Ehcache framework also supports replication using JGroups. Similar to the RMI-based Ehcache replication, Liferay also supports JGroup-based replication. Let's learn how to configure the JGroup-based Ehcache replication.

1. Stop both the Liferay Portal nodes if they are running.
2. Add the following properties to the `portal-ext.properties` file of both the Liferay Portal nodes:

   ```
   ehcache.multi.vm.config.location=/ehcache/liferay-multi-vm-clustered.xml
   ehcache.multi.vm.config.location.peerProviderProperties=connect=UDP(mcast_addr=multicast.group.address["hibernate"];mcast_port=multicast.group.port["hibernate"];):PING:MERGE2:FD_SOCK:VERIFY_SUSPECT:pbcast.NAKACK:UNICAST:pbcast.STABLE:FRAG:pbcast.GMS
   ehcache.bootstrap.cache.loader.factory=com.liferay.portal.cache.ehcache.JGroupsBootstrapCacheLoaderFactory
   ehcache.cache.event.listener.factory=net.sf.ehcache.distribution.jgroups.JGroupsCacheReplicatorFactory
   net.sf.ehcache.configurationResourceName=/ehcache/hibernate-clustered.xml
   net.sf.ehcache.configurationResourceName.peerProviderProperties=peerDiscovery=connect=UDP(mcast_addr=multicast.group.address["multi-vm"];mcast_port=multicast.group.port["multi-vm"];):PING:MERGE2:FD_SOCK:VERIFY_SUSPECT:pbcast.NAKACK:UNICAST:pbcast.STABLE:FRAG:pbcast.GMS
   multicast.group.address["hibernate"]=233.0.0.4
   multicast.group.port["hibernate"]=23304
   multicast.group.address["multi-vm"]=233.0.0.5
   multicast.group.port["multi-vm"]=23305
   ```

3. Now restart both the nodes one by one to activate the preceding configuration.

The Ehcache replication configuration is very similar to the RMI-based replication. Here, we used the UDP protocol to connect Liferay Portal nodes. With this option both Liferay Portal nodes also connect with each other using IP multicast.

Ehcache replication using Cluster Links

We learned about the JGroups- and RMI-based Ehcache replication. The Liferay Enterprise version includes another powerful feature called **Cluster Link**, which provides the Ehcache replication mechanism. Internally, this feature uses JGroups to replicate the cache across the network. Let's go through the steps to configure this feature.

1. Stop both the Liferay Portal nodes if they are running.
2. Now deploy the `ehcache-cluster-web` enterprise plugin on both the Liferay Portal servers.
3. Now, edit `portal-ext.properties` of both the nodes:
   `cluster.link.enabled=true`
   `ehcache.cluster.link.replication.enabled=true`
   `net.sf.ehcache.configurationResourceName=/ehcache/hibernate-clustered.xml`
   `ehcache.multi.vm.config.location=/ehcache/liferay-multi-vm-clustered.xml`
4. Now restart both the Liferay Portal servers to activate this configuration.

In *Chapter 1, Architectural Best Practices*, we talked about this option. Unlike the JGroups- or RMI-based Ehcache replication, this option centralizes all Ehcache changes at one place and then distributes changes to all the nodes of the cluster. This in turn reduces unnecessary network transfers.

> This option is only available in the Liferay Enterprise version. Hence, the preceding steps are applicable only if you are using the Liferay Enterprise version.

Ehcache clustering best practices

We talked about different options to configure Ehcache replication. Let's learn the best practices related to Ehcache replication.

- If there are more than two nodes in the cluster, it is recommended to either use Cluster Link- or JGroups-based replication. If we are using the Liferay Enterprise edition, it is recommended to use Cluster Link for Ehcache replication.
- All three options that we discussed previously use IP multicast for establishing connections with other nodes. The IP multicast technique uses group IP and port to know other nodes in the same group. It is very important to ensure that the same IP and port are used by the nodes of the same cluster.

- It is advisable to keep the group IP and port different for development, testing, or staging environment to make sure that the nodes of other environments do not pair up with the production environment.
- Cluster Link provides up to 10 transport channels to transfer cached resources across the cluster. If the application is supposed to have a huge cache and frequent cache changes, it is advisable to configure multiple transport channels using the `cluster.link.channel.properties.transport` configuration property.

Media Library configuration

Media Library is one of the most important features of Liferay Portal. The Media Library content is divided into two repositories. The metadata of the Media Library content is stored in the Liferay database. The actual media files are stored by default on the filesystem. For a clustered setup, we need to make sure that the media files are stored in a centralized repository, otherwise each node will have their own copy of files. Liferay Portal provides various options to store media files in centralized storage. Let's learn how to configure Media Library for the clustered environment and then talk about best practices.

Network file storage using the Advanced File System store

In *Chapter 1, Architectural Best Practices*, we talked about the Advanced File System store. It's a pluggable Media Library repository store. It stores files on the filesystem, but it divides files into multiple directories. This feature improves the efficiency in locating the files, especially when the files are stored on the network filesystem. To use this option in a clustered environment, we need to use a Storage Area Network appliance or Network File System. We need to mount the storage SAN or the NFS directory on both the Liferay Portal nodes. Let's learn how to configure Media Library with the Advanced File System store.

1. Stop both the Liferay Portal nodes if they are running.
2. Add the following properties to `portal-ext.properties` of both the Liferay Portal nodes:

   ```
   dl.store.impl=com.liferay.portlet.documentlibrary.store.AdvancedFileSystemStore
   dl.store.file.system.root.dir=<SAN Directory>
   ```

3. Now restart both the Liferay Portal nodes one by one.

We have configured Media Library to use `AdvancedFileSystemStore`, and also provided a networked location where the Portal should store the Media Library content. Both the Portal nodes will store content in the same filesystem location. To use this option, we need to make sure the SAN appliance supports file locking, as multiple nodes will access the filesystem at the same time. As this option requires specialized hardware like SAN or NFS, it will add additional cost to the solution.

Database storage using the JCR store

Liferay Portal provides an option to store the Media Library content to the database using the JCR store. Liferay Portal uses Apache Jackrabbit as JCR implementation. Jackrabbit provides both filesystem- and database-based storage for the content. By default, the Jackrabbit configuration uses filesystem-based storage. Another option is to configure Jackrabbit to use the database for the Media Library content. Let's learn how to configure Media Library using the JCR store.

1. Stop both the Liferay Portal nodes if they are already running.

2. Edit `portal-ext.properties` of both the nodes and add the following configuration:

   ```
   dl.store.impl=com.liferay.portlet.documentlibrary.store.JCRStore
   ```

3. Now edit `node-01\liferay-portal-6.1.1-ce-ga2\data\jackrabbit\repository.xml` and make the following changes:

    1. Comment the following lines from the file:

       ```xml
       <FileSystem class="org.apache.jackrabbit.core.fs.local.LocalFileSystem">
       <param name="path" value="${rep.home}/repository" />
       </FileSystem>
       ```

    2. Uncomment the following lines and change the values as given in the following code snippet. Make sure you provide the correct IP, username, and password of the MySQL database:

       ```xml
       <FileSystem class="org.apache.jackrabbit.core.fs.db.DbFileSystem">
       <param name="driver" value="com.mysql.jdbc.Driver"/>
       <param name="url" value="jdbc:mysql:// {IP of MySQL Database Server}/lportal"/>
       <param name="schema" value="mysql"/>
       <param name="user" value="{Database User Id}"/>
       <param name="password" value="{Database Password}"/>
       <param name="schemaObjectPrefix" value="J_R_FS_"/>
       </FileSystem>
       ```

3. Comment the following lines that appear within the `<workspace>` tag:

```xml
<FileSystem class="org.apache.jackrabbit.core.fs.local.
LocalFileSystem">
   <param name="path" value="${wsp.home}" />
</FileSystem>
<PersistenceManager class="org.apache.jackrabbit.core.
persistence.bundle.BundleFsPersistenceManager" />
```

4. Uncomment and change the following lines that appear within the `<workspace>` tag. Make sure you provide the correct IP, username, and password of the MySQL database:

```xml
<PersistenceManager class="org.apache.jackrabbit.core.state.
db.SimpleDbPersistenceManager">
<param name="driver" value="com.mysql.jdbc.Driver" />
<param name="url" value="jdbc:mysql:// {IP of MySQL Database
Server}/lportal" />
<param name="user" value="{Database User Id}"/>
<param name="password" value="{Database Password}"/>
<param name="schema" value="mysql" />
<param name="schemaObjectPrefix" value="J_PM_${wsp.name}_"
/>
<param name="externalBLOBs" value="false" />
</PersistenceManager>
<FileSystem class="org.apache.jackrabbit.core.fs.db.
DbFileSystem">
<param name="driver" value="com.mysql.jdbc.Driver"/>
<param name="url" value="jdbc:mysql:// {IP of MySQL Database
Server}/lportal" />
<param name="user" value="{Database User Id}"/>
<param name="password" value="{Database Password}"/>
<param name="schema" value="mysql"/>
<param name="schemaObjectPrefix" value="J_FS_${wsp.name}_"/>
</FileSystem>
```

5. Uncomment the following lines of code within the `<versioning>` tag:

```xml
<FileSystem class="org.apache.jackrabbit.core.fs.local.
LocalFileSystem">
<param name="path" value="${rep.home}/version" />
</FileSystem>
<PersistenceManager class="org.apache.jackrabbit.core.
persistence.bundle.BundleFsPersistenceManager"/>
```

6. Uncomment the following lines that appear within the `<Versioning>` tag. Make sure you provide the correct IP, username, and password of the MySQL database:

```
<FileSystem class="org.apache.jackrabbit.core.fs.db.DbFileSystem">
<param name="driver" value="com.mysql.jdbc.Driver"/>
<param name="url" value="jdbc:mysql:// {IP of MySQL Database Server}/lportal" />
<param name="user" value="{Database User Id}"/>
<param name="password" value="{Database Password}"/>
<param name="schema" value="mysql"/>
<param name="schemaObjectPrefix" value="J_V_FS_"/>
</FileSystem>
<PersistenceManager class="org.apache.jackrabbit.core.state.db.SimpleDbPersistenceManager">
<param name="driver" value="com.mysql.jdbc.Driver" />
<param name="url" value="jdbc:mysql:// {IP of MySQL Database Server}/lportal" />
<param name="user" value="{Database User Id}"/>
<param name="password" value="{Database Password}"/>
<param name="schema" value="mysql" />
<param name="schemaObjectPrefix" value="J_V_PM_" />
<param name="externalBLOBs" value="false" />
</PersistenceManager>
```

7. Finally, uncomment and change the following tag within the `<Clustering>` tag. Make sure you provide the correct IP, username, and password of the MySQL database:

```
<Cluster id="node_1" syncDelay="5">
<Journal class="org.apache.jackrabbit.core.journal.DatabaseJournal">
<param name="revision" value="${rep.home}/revision"/>
<param name="driver" value="com.mysql.jdbc.Driver"/>
<param name="url" value="jdbc:mysql:// {IP of MySQL Database Server}/lportal"/>
<param name="user" value="{Database User Id}"/>
<param name="password" value="{Database Password}"/>
<param name="schema" value="mysql"/>
<param name="schemaObjectPrefix" value="J_C_"/>
</Journal>
</Cluster>
```

4. Now, replace the same file in the other node and change the `id` attribute of the `cluster` tag to `node_2`.
5. Restart both the Liferay Portal nodes one by one.

In the preceding configuration, we first enabled the JCR store for Media Library. This change will internally use Jackrabbit to store the Media Library content. By default, configuration of Jackrabbit is stored in the `repository.xml` file. By default, the Jackrabbit configuration stores the Media Library content in the data folder. We configured the `repository.xml` file to store content in the same `lportal` database. We can also configure the `repository.xml` file such that it stores the Media Library content in a separate database. Jackrabbit internally divides the Media Library data into the following types of data in the database:

- Repository-filesystem-related data
- Workspace-related data
- Versioning-related data
- Cluster-related data

We configured the `repository.xml` file such that the preceding data is stored in the database.

Database storage using DBStore

Liferay Portal 6.1 introduced a new type of repository store to persist Media Library content in the Liferay database. It is very simple to configure and provides better performance than the JCR store with the database. Let's learn how to configure Media Library to use `DBStore`.

1. Stop both the Liferay Portal nodes if they are already running.
2. Edit `portal-ext.properties` of both the nodes and add the following configuration:
   ```
   dl.store.impl= com.liferay.portlet.documentlibrary.store.DBStore
   ```
3. Restart both the Liferay Portal nodes one by one.

Media Library clustering best practices

We talked about two options to centralize Media Library content storage. In *Chapter 1, Architectural Best Practices*, we briefly talked about other options too. Let's talk about some of the best practices related to Media Library.

- In a clustered environment, the filesystem-based Media Library store can only be used with SAN or NFS that supports file locking.

- If the Media Library content needs to be stored in the database, DBStore is preferred over the JCR store with database. DB Store is better for performance and scalability.
- If JCR-based database storage is used for Media Library, it is recommended to keep the JCR database separate.
- If JCR-based database storage is used for Media Library, it is very important to ensure that the cluster node ID is unique in the Jackrabbit configuration file (repository.xml).

Search engine configuration

Liferay Portal uses Apache Lucene as a search engine. Apache Lucene creates search indexes to provide the search functionality. Apache Lucene, by default, stores search indexes into the filesystem. To make sure the search functionality works properly in a clustered environment, we need to synchronize search indexes of all the Liferay Portal nodes. There are multiple options to make sure the search functionality works properly in a clustered environment. Let's learn how to configure these options and then talk about the best practices associated with them.

Lucene index storage on network storage

Liferay's Lucene configuration provides a way to configure the index storage directory through the portal-ext.properties file. In order to use this option, we will need a specialized Storage Area Network (SAN) appliance with file locking capabilities. Let's learn how to configure Lucene to store index files on the SAN appliance.

1. Stop both the Liferay Portal servers if they are already running.
2. Add the following property to portal-ext.properties of both the Liferay Portal nodes:

   lucene.dir=<SAN based mapped directory>

3. Now start both the nodes one by one.
4. Now, access the Portal and sign in using admin user name. Then from the dock bar, access **Control Panel** and then from the **Server Administration** section, click on the button beside the **Rebuild all search indexes** label.

We have just added a property in the portal-ext.properties file that specifies the location of the search indexes. Both the Liferay Portal nodes will specify the same network storage directory and hence, both the nodes will refer to the same copy of search indexes. As the index storage location has changed, we rebuilt search indexes for the existing data. This is the easiest option to centralize search indexes.

Lucene index replication using Cluster Link

We talked about the Cluster Link feature for Ehcache replication. Cluster Link is a very powerful feature and it can be used for Lucene index replication as well. Using Cluster Link, Liferay Portal sends index changes to all the other Liferay Portal nodes in the group. Internally, Cluster Links uses JGroups to send the index data across to other nodes. Let's learn how to configure Cluster Link to replicate search indexes.

1. Stop both the Liferay Portal nodes if they are already running.
2. Add the following properties to the `portal-ext.properties` file of both the nodes:

   ```
   cluster.link.enabled=true
   lucene.replicate.write=true
   ```

3. Now restart both the nodes one by one.

We simply enabled Cluster Link through `portal-ext.properties`. We enable one of the Lucene properties which generates replication events through Cluster Link for every search index change. Cluster Link then distributes the event to all the nodes in the cluster. With this option, each node will have their copy of search indexes.

Using the Apache Solr search engine

Apache Solr is one of the powerful open search engine projects. Liferay supports Apache Solr integration. We can replace the default Lucene search engine with Solr. Unlike Lucene, Solr runs as a separate application. In a clustered environment, Liferay Portal nodes connect to centralize the Solr server to search and index the data. Let's learn how to configure Liferay Portal with Solr.

1. Connect to the server on which Solr has to be installed and create a root named `Solr`.
2. Download Apache Tomcat 7.0.34 server from the `http://apache.techartifact.com/mirror/tomcat/tomcat-7/v7.0.34/bin/apache-tomcat-7.0.34.zip` URL.
3. Extract the `apache-tomcat-7.0.34.zip` file in the `solr` directory.
4. Download Apache Solr 1.4.0 from the `http://archive.apache.org/dist/lucene/solr/1.4.0/apache-solr-1.4.0.zip` URL.
5. Extract the preceding `apache-solr-1.4.0.zip` file to a temporary directory. From the extracted directory, copy the content of the `apache-solr-1.4.0/example/solr` directory to the `solr` directory created in step 1.

6. In the preceding temporary directory, you can locate the Apache Solr WAR file in the apache-solr-1.4.0/dist directory. Rename the WAR file to solr.war and copy it to the solr/apache-tomcat-7.0.34/webapps directory.

7. In the catalina.sh file, add the JVM argument for -Dsolr.solr.home=<fully qualified path of solr directory created in step 1>.

8. Start the Solr Tomcat server and access Solr Admin using the http://localhost:8080/solr/admin URL.

9. Now from the Liferay Marketplace, download the Solr Search Engine CE app. Liferay Marketplace can be accessed from the http://www.liferay.com/marketplace URL. From the Marketplace, we will get a file with the .lpkg extension.

10. Now, copy this file to deploy the directory of both the nodes and start them. By default, the deployed directory will be there in the liferay-portal-6.1.1-ce-ga2 directory.

11. On startup, both the Liferay nodes will deploy the solr-web plugin.

12. Once the solr-web plugin is deployed successfully, stop both the nodes again.

13. Now edit node-01\liferay-portal-6.1.1-ce-ga2\ tomcat-7.0.27\webapps\solr-web\WEB-INF\classes\META-INF\solr-spring.xml and change the Solr server URL as follows:

```
<bean id="com.liferay.portal.search.solr.server.BasicAuthSolrServer" class="com.liferay.portal.search.solr.server.BasicAuthSolrServer">
<constructor-arg type="java.lang.String" value="http://localhost:8080/solr" />
</bean>
```

14. Make the same changes in liferay-node-02.

15. Now on the Solr server, replace the solr/conf/schema.xml file with the node-01/liferay-portal-6.1.1-ce-ga2/tomcat-7.0.27/webapps/solr-web/WEB-INF/conf/schema.xml file from liferay-node-01.

16. Now restart the Solr Tomcat server. Then, restart both the Liferay Portal nodes.

We just configured Solr 1.4 as a separate application on the Tomcat server. We then deployed the `solr-web` plugin on both the nodes. The `solr-web` plugin connects to the Solr server. We configured the URL of our Solr server by changing the spring configuration file. The Solr server uses a predefined schema for indexes. Liferay Portal has its own schema for indexes. This schema file is supplied with the `solr-web` plugin. We replaced the Solr server schema with the one provided with the `solr-web` plugin. After the preceding setup, when we create any data like a user or blog, indexes of related data will be created in the Solr server.

Clustering best practices for the search engine

We learned about three options available to configure the search engine to work properly in a clustered environment. Let's learn some of the best practices associated with them.

- If the Portal application is expected to write a few indexes, it is recommended to use the Cluster Link option. It is a lightweight option and can be configured quickly.

- As indexes are accessed and changed frequently, a network filesystem-based index storage can create issues related to concurrent file access. Hence, it is advisable to avoid using that option even though it gives the best performance.

- If the Portal application is expected to have a large amount of data written to search indexes, it is advisable to use the Solr search engine instead of other options.

- The Solr server provides a master/slave server concept. If the Portal application is expected to have a huge amount of read and write transactions on search indexes, it is advisable to use that option to manage heavy loads.

- If the Cluster Link option is used to replicate search indexes and the Portal application is expected to have frequent index changes, it is advisable to configure multiple transport channels for the Cluster Link.

Quartz scheduler configuration

Liferay Portal includes a built-in scheduler engine. There are many features in Liferay Portal that use a scheduler; for example, expiration of web content, LDAP import functionality, and so on. Liferay also supports setting up a scheduler for custom portlets. Internally, Liferay Portal uses the Quartz scheduler. Quartz is a very popular open source scheduler engine. Quartz scheduler stores data related to scheduled jobs in the Liferay database. Hence in a clustered environment, it is possible that multiple nodes start the same job at the same time. This can create havoc. To prevent this situation, we need to configure Quartz for the clustered environment.

Let's learn how to configure the Quartz scheduler to run in the clustered environment.

1. Stop both the Liferay Portal servers if they are running.
2. Add the following property to the `portal-ext.properties` file of both the Liferay Portal nodes:

   `org.quartz.jobStore.isClustered=true`
3. From the `lportal` database, drop all the tables starting with `QUARTZ_`. This step is required if Liferay tables are already created.
4. Now restart both the Liferay Portal servers.

We just added a property to let the Quartz scheduler know that we are running multiple instances of the Quartz scheduler connected to a single database. By enabling this property, the Quartz scheduler will make sure that each job is executed only once.

Summary

We have learned how to configure Liferay Portal in the clustered environment. We also learned how to configure the software load balancer using the Apache Web Server. We talked about various options and best practices related to load balancing and clustering configuration. We covered how to configure Media Library, search engine, cache, and scheduler to work in the clustered environment. With this knowledge, we can decide the best options to configure a load balanced and clustered environment.

Let's get ready to learn various configuration best practices to set up a high-performing Liferay Portal.

3
Configuration Best Practices

In *Chapter 2*, *Load Balancing and Clustering Best Practices*, we learned about clustering and load balancing best practices. We learned about the configuration of various components for load balancing and clustering. In *Chapter 1*, *Architectural Best Practices*, we learned about the reference architecture of a Liferay-Portal-based solution and its various components. All of these components are configurable and allow us to change their behavior according to our requirements. In this chapter, we will focus on the configuration settings that can improve the performance of the overall solution. We will also talk about the consequences of applying various configuration settings.

By the end of this chapter, we will learn about the following topics:

- Liferay Portal configuration best practices
    - Servlet filter configuration
    - Service bus configuration
    - Optional features configuration
    - Lucene configuration
    - Scheduler configuration

- Application Server configuration best practices
    - JVM configuration
    - Thread pool configuration
    - Other Application Server configurations

- Apache Web Server configuration best practices
    - Static content delivery
    - GZip compression configuration
    - Cache header configuration
    - MPM configuration

Liferay Portal configuration best practices

In this section, we will learn the various Liferay Portal configuration settings for achieving best performance. These configuration settings are categorized into multiple sections. Let's learn these configuration settings in detail.

Servlet filter configuration

Liferay Portal ships with a bunch of features which are implemented using servlet filters. An example of such feature includes NTLM SSO integration, CAS SSO integration, SharePoint integration, and so on. Irrespective of whether we are using such features, all requests pass through a chain of filters depending upon the filter configuration. So, a fraction of CPU and memory will be consumed by some of the unnecessary filters for every request. Liferay Portal provides a way to disable these features. In this section, we will learn about these filters in detail. We will also learn how to disable them to improve performance.

The auto login filter

Liferay Portal implements the auto login feature using the auto login filter. The auto login feature is used to sign in to the Portal automatically without using the traditional sign-in mechanism. For example, if we want to sign in to Liferay Portal by passing the username and password in URL requests, we will need to bypass the traditional sign-in form. This feature intercepts every secure request using the HTTP servlet filter. The auto login functionality is implemented using the hook-based mechanism to allow customizations. The auto login filter delegates every request to a chain of auto login hooks. If any of the auto login hooks return a success result, it automatically signs the user in. By default, the auto login filter is used for the following features:

- CAS SSO integration
- Facebook SSO integration
- NTLM SSO integration
- OpenID SSO integration
- OpenSSO integration
- Site Minder SSO integration
- The Remember Me feature (saves login information using the Remember Me checkbox in the Sign in portlet)

The auto login filter is also used when we define a custom auto login hook through `portal-ext.properties`. If we are not using the auto login functionality in the portal, it is recommended to disable the auto login filter. By disabling this filter, we can improve the response time and load on the Portal's server. To disable this filter, we need to add the following property in the `portal-ext.properties` file:

```
com.liferay.portal.servlet.filters.autologin.AutoLoginFilter=false
```

The CAS filter

Central Authentication Service (CAS) is an authentication system. Liferay Portal supports Single Sign-on with CAS. As discussed in the previous section, most of the SSO integrations in Liferay Portal are implemented using servlet filters. For CAS integration, Liferay Portal includes the CAS filter. This filter intercepts all secure requests. It redirects all the unauthenticated secure requests to the CAS server for authentication. Even when we are not using CAS integration, all secure requests will pass through this filter. It is recommended to disable this filter if we are not using it. To disable this filter, we need to add following property to the `portal-ext.properties` file:

```
com.liferay.portal.servlet.filters.sso.cas.CASFilter=false
```

The NTLM SSO filter

NTLM is a Windows protocol, which provides an authentication service. Liferay provides support to authenticate users using NTLM. With this feature, users do not need to sign in to Liferay Portal to access secure pages. The system automatically authenticates the user based on their Windows login credentials. This feature is also implemented using servlet filters. If this feature is not used, it is recommended to disable the servlet filters to improve the response time. To disable filters associated with this feature, we need to add the following properties in `portal-ext.properties`:

```
com.liferay.portal.servlet.filters.sso.ntlm.NtlmFilter=false
com.liferay.portal.servlet.filters.sso.ntlm.NtlmPostFilter=false
```

The OpenSSO filter

OpenSSO is one of the leading open source SSO providers. It is now known as **OpenAM**. Liferay supports integration with OpenSSO. OpenSSO integration is also implemented using the servlet filter. Again, if OpenSSO is not used, it is recommended to disable the servlet filter. This can be done by adding the following property to `portal-ext.properties`:

```
com.liferay.portal.servlet.filters.sso.opensso.OpenSSOFilter=false
```

The SharePoint filter

Liferay Portal supports accessing documents from Media Gallery through the SharePoint protocol. Using this feature, we can directly access Media Gallery documents in MS Office. This feature is implemented using the servlet filter. If we are not using this feature, it is recommended to disable the SharePoint filter to improve performance. This can be done by adding the following property to `portal-ext.properties`:

```
com.liferay.portal.sharepoint.SharepointFilter=false
```

The GZip filter

It is a common technique to compress HTTP responses using GZip compression to improve the response time by reducing network data transfer time. Liferay Portal also supports this technique. Liferay implements this feature using the GZip filter. Although this feature benefits by reducing the size of response, it uses server resources to compress the response. If we are using the Apache Web server in front of the Liferay Portal server, it is a good idea to compress the response on the Apache Web Server. GZip compression on the Apache Web Server gives a better performance than the Liferay Portal server. Hence, it is recommended to disable this feature in Liferay and enable GZip compression in the Apache Web Server. This feature can be disabled by adding the following property to `portal-ext.properties`:

```
com.liferay.portal.servlet.filters.gzip.GZipFilter=false
```

The Strip filter

Liferay provides a feature to remove blank lines from the generated response. This feature is implemented using the Strip filter. It reduces the size of responses and ultimately, helps in improving the network data transfer time. But it increases processing on the Liferay Portal server for every request. We can remove blank lines from the compiled JSP files by using the Tomcat server configuration. It doesn't add any extra processing overhead. Hence, it is recommended to disable this filter if it is possible to remove blank lines using Tomcat configuration. To disable this filter, we need to add the following property to `portal-ext.properties`:

```
com.liferay.portal.servlet.filters.strip.StripFilter=false
```

The ValidHtml filter

It is a common technique to add JavaScript out of the body tag to improve the page rendering performance. But theoretically, it creates an invalid HTML response. Because of this screen, readers cannot access the response. This filter moves JavaScript files within the HTML body tag. This filter adds overhead for every request. It is recommended to keep this filter disabled to improve performance. This can be done by adding the following property to portal-ext.properties:

```
com.liferay.portal.servlet.filters.validhtml.ValidHtmlFilter=false
```

Auto login hooks

In the previous section, we talked about the auto login functionality. This functionality is implemented using the auto login filter and auto login hooks. As discussed earlier, if we are not using any of the auto login features, we can disable the auto login filter. But if we are using any of the auto login functionality, we cannot disable the auto login filter. In that scenario, the auto login filter will process all the auto login hooks to perform auto login. So, it will process some of the unnecessary auto login hooks as well. Liferay Portal provides a way to configure only the required hooks. This can be configured by removing unnecessary hooks from the following property:

```
auto.login.hooks=com.liferay.portal.security.auth.CASAutoLogin,com.liferay.portal.security.auth.FacebookAutoLogin,com.liferay.portal.security.auth.NtlmAutoLogin,com.liferay.portal.security.auth.OpenIdAutoLogin,com.liferay.portal.security.auth.OpenSSOAutoLogin,com.liferay.portal.security.auth.RememberMeAutoLogin,com.liferay.portal.security.auth.SiteMinderAutoLogin
```

As shown in the property, by default, many auto login hooks are configured. We should keep only the required auto login hooks and then add this property to portal-ext.properties. It will improve the performance by removing unnecessary processing for each secure request.

Counter increment

Liferay Portal uses counter services for generating unique IDs. Most of the built-in and custom persistence services developed using service builder use counter service to generate unique IDs. Counter services persist counters in the database table. Counter services always communicate with the database to reserve counter values. So once the reserved counter values are used, Liferay Portal again invokes database queries and gets the next set of reserve values.

Liferay Portal provides a way to configure a number of reserve counters to be maintained in the memory. By default, the reserve counter value is 100. So once 100 counters are used, the system will make a database call and get the next 100 counters. If the application is used to generate a large amount of data and it is using the counter service for generating such data, it is recommend to set a higher value for this counter. For production systems, it is recommended to configure the counter value to 2000. We can configure the counter value by adding the following property to `portal-ext.properties`:

```
counter.increment=2000
```

The counter service also allows us to define unique counters by the specific category. For example, we can maintain separate counters for the `Layout` service. To do that, we need to provide the counter category name while generating the new counter. For such cases, we can even specify the counter increment value by adding the category name after `counter.increment` in `portal-ext.properties`. For example, Liferay maintains separate counters for `Layout` services. To specify different increment values for `Layout` services, we can add the following property to `portal-ext.properties`:

```
counter.increment.com.liferay.portal.model.Layout=10
```

User session tracker

Liferay provides a feature for administrators to view user session activities. It allows admin users to look at what a user is doing on the Portal. It is a great feature for debugging and troubleshooting. But to capture user session activities, it uses a high amount of server resources. It is recommended to disable this feature in the production environment. To disable this feature, we need to add the following entry to `portal-ext.properties`:

```
session.tracker.memory.enabled=false
```

Direct Servlet Context

Liferay includes a feature to speed up the loading of JSP files within Liferay's tag libraries. Liferay's tag classes are used to dispatch requests to the JSP file. Dispatching a request to the JSP file involves resource look up. It also involves execution of the filter chain. This can be avoided for the tag libraries. To solve this issue, Liferay uses the Direct Servlet Context mechanism. This feature improves the performance of Liferay tag libraries. This feature also includes a developer-friendly capability that checks for JSP modifications. Because of this capability, the system always checks for the last modified date of the JSP pages. This capability is useful for developers but may not be required for the production environment.

Fortunately, Liferay provides a way to enable or disable this check through configuration. It is recommended to disable this check in the production environment. We can disable this check by adding the following property to `portal-ext.properties`:

```
direct.servlet.context.reload=false
```

Plugin repositories

Liferay Portal uses online plugin repositories to check for updates. Liferay provides a way to configure which plugin repositories it should check for. Internally, Liferay runs a scheduler every day, which reloads all the configured repositories. This check involves accessing the repository using the repository URL. It also checks for the new version of the installed plugins. In the production environment, we usually avoid making direct installations. Hence, this feature is not really useful in the production environment. But still it consumes resources every day to download the metadata of the configured plugin repositories. It is recommended to disable these features in the production environment. To disable these features, we need to add the following properties to `portal-ext.properties`:

```
plugin.repositories.trusted=
plugin.repositories.untrusted=
plugin.notifications.enabled=false
```

Pingbacks and trackbacks

Pingbacks and trackbacks are methods to request a notification when somebody adds the link of a web resource to their documents. Liferay supports trackbacks and pingbacks for collaboration features like blogs and message boards. Liferay Portal provides a way to configure the trackback and pingback URLs for each blog and message board posts. Internally, Liferay Portal sends requests to the pingback and trackback URLs. This operation uses a good amount of server resources. If the solution uses blogs and message board portlets but it does not need the pingback and trackback features, the system will unnecessarily use system resources for these features. Liferay Portal provides a way to disable these features. To disable them we need to add the following properties to `portal-ext.properties`:

```
#
# Todisable pingbacks in blogs portlet.
#
blogs.pingback.enabled=false
#
# Todisable trackbacks in blogs portlet.
#
blogs.trackback.enabled=false
```

```
#
# Todisable pingbacks in message board portlet.
#
message.boards.pingback.enabled=false
```

Google's blog search ping integration

Google provides a search service for blogs. We can search any blog using Google's blog search service. To ensure a particular blog to appear in Google's blog search, Google provides a **ping** service. This service is used to make sure that the blogs are indexed by the Google blog search. Liferay Portal provides integration with Google's blog search ping service. This integration internally calls Google's ping service when a blog is created or updated. If the portal solution does not require Google blog search integration, it is recommended to disable this option for better performance. This feature can be disabled by adding the following property to `portal-ext.properties`:

```
blogs.ping.google.enabled=false
```

The asset view counter

Liferay uses the Asset framework for its content management system. Each web content in Liferay is an Asset. Liferay provides a feature to maintain a view counter for each asset. This feature ensures incrementing the view counter whenever the asset is viewed from any of the portlets. Liferay maintains the view counter in the database. Hence to maintain the view counter, internally, Liferay Portal executes update queries. For each access of the page or asset, it will execute the update query. This feature increases the load on the Database and Application servers, even for the read-only access. If the Portal solution does not require the knowledge of the view count of assets, it is recommended to disable this option. It can improve the response time and performance of the system. To disable this feature, we need to add the following property to `portal-ext.properties`:

```
asset.entry.increment.view.counter.enabled=false
```

Document ranks and view count

The Media Library portlet of Liferay provides a feature to record the download rank and view count for documents. Whenever a document is downloaded or viewed, it increments the view counter and the download rank. The recent download portlet lists documents based on the document rank. Similarly, we can enable displaying the view count in the Documents and Media display portlet. These features update the data in the database whenever documents are downloaded or viewed. If these features are not used in the portal, it is recommended to disable them. It will reduce the load on the Database and Application Servers.

To disable these features, we need to add the following properties to `portal-ext.properties`:

```
#
# To disable file rank for document library files.
#
dl.file.rank.enabled=false
#
# To disable the read count for document library files.
#
dl.file.entry.read.count.enabled=false
```

Scheduler configuration

Liferay Portal provides built-in integration with the Quartz scheduler. Many of the Liferay features use a scheduler. Depending upon the feature and its configuration, the scheduled jobs are executed in the background. These background jobs run on the same Liferay Portal servers. Hence, these jobs will use the Portal server resources. Scheduled jobs are executed for all the features irrespective of whether they are used or not. They may finish quickly but will consume some of the system resources. Hence, it is advisable to disable schedulers associated with unused features. The following built-in features use schedulers in Liferay Portal:

- The Calendar portlet
- LDAP integration
- The Web Content portlet
- The Message Board portlet
- The Blogs portlet
- The Media Library portlet
- The Announcement portlet

The Calendar portlet

Liferay's Calendar portlet uses a scheduler to send reminders for events. If the Calendar portlet or event reminder feature is not used, it is recommended to disable the scheduler job created for the Calendar portlet. To disable the scheduler used in the Calendar portlet, we need to add the following property to `portal-ext.properties`:

```
calendar.event.check.interval=-1
```

LDAP integration

Liferay Portal provides built-in integration with LDAP. Liferay Portal uses the scheduler to import users from the LDAP server to the Liferay Portal server. From the Control Panel, we can configure whether to import users from LDAP or not. But even though we disable the LDAP import, Liferay Portal runs the scheduler and exists if it finds that the LDAP import is disabled. So in any scenario, the scheduler job will get executed. If the LDAP import is not used, it is recommended to disable the LDAP import scheduler itself to save server resources. This can be done by adding the following property to `portal-ext.properties`:

```
ldap.import.interval=-1
```

The Web Content portlet

Liferay Portal provides a way to configure future expiration and review the date for web content. In order to expire the web content and send ane-mail on the review date, Liferay Portal uses a scheduler. If web content is not used, or web content is never going to be expired or reviewed, it is recommended to disable the Web Content portlet scheduler. This will improve the performance of the Application Server. This scheduler can be disabled by adding the following property to `portal-ext.properties`:

```
journal.article.check.interval=-1
```

The Message Board portlet

The Message Board portlet provides a feature to ban users from accessing the Message Board portlet. Liferay Portal runs a scheduler to unban the banned user after a certain interval. If the Message Board portlet is not used or the ban user functionality is not used, it is recommended to disable this scheduler. To disable this scheduler, we need to add the following property to `portal-ext.properties`:

```
message.boards.expire.ban.job.interval=-1
```

The Blogs portlet

As discussed earlier, the Blogs portlet supports pingbacks and trackbacks. Liferay Portal implements these features by using scheduler. Even if we disable these features as discussed earlier, the system will still execute scheduled jobs. It is recommended to disable the scheduler associated with these features if they are not used. The Blogs portlet also provides the facility to publish blogs on future dates. This feature is also implemented using scheduler. The scheduler will change the status of the blog on the display date. We can also disable the scheduler associated with this feature using the configuration. To disable these schedulers, we need to add the following properties to `portal-ext.properties`:

```
blogs.linkback.job.interval=-1
blogs.entry.check.interval=-1
```

The Media Library portlet

The Media Library portlet provides a feature to rank documents based on downloads. Media Library maintains the top *n* ranks. It doesn't give a rank to every document. Hence to maintain the top *n* ranked documents, the system has to clean up data in the document rank table. This clean up feature is implemented using the scheduler. It is recommended to disable this scheduler if the file ranking feature is not used. This can be done by adding the following property to `portal-ext.properties`:

```
dl.file.rank.check.interval=-1
```

The Announcement portlet

The Announcement portlet provides a way to notify the user about the announcement using e-mails. This feature is implemented using a scheduler. If the Announcement or Alerts portlet is not used in the solution, it is recommended to disable this scheduler. It can be done by adding the following entry to `portal-ext.properties`:

```
announcements.entry.check.interval=-1
```

We looked at the features of Liferay Portal that are using scheduler and learned how to disable them. If none of the preceding features are used and none of the customer portlets uses a scheduler, it is recommended to disable the scheduler itself in Liferay Portal. This can be done by adding the following property to `portal-ext.properties`:

```
scheduler.enabled=false
```

Inline permission checks

Since version 6, Liferay Portal has implemented database query-driven permission checks while browsing or searching content. This permission check affects the performance of the system because of heavy database queries. On the other side, it is useful for mainly social collaboration features. If the Portal is not using social collaboration features, we should switch off the inline permission check to improve the performance of the system. Fortunately, Liferay provides a way to disable the inline permission check using configuration. We need to add the following property to `portal-ext.properties` to disable the inline permission check:

```
permissions.inline.sql.check.enabled=false
```

Lucene Configuration

As discussed earlier, Liferay uses Apache Lucene as a search engine. If the Portal is heavily using search functionalities, it is required to tune the Lucene search engine. We can tune the Lucene configuration parameters from `portal-ext.properties`. The Lucene engine internally maintains index changes in memory and at certain intervals persists index changes on the filesystem. If the Portal is designed to create a large amount of indexes, one of the important configuration is how often we commit index changes to the filesystem. By default, Liferay is configured to commit every index change on the filesystem. For a large number of index writes, it will slow down the system. It is recommended to configure the following parameters in the `portal-ext.properties` file as starting values and tune them during a load test:

```
#Set the value of batch size to configure how many consecutive
#updates will trigger a commit to file.
lucene.commit.batch.size=10000

#Set the commit time interval in milliseconds after which commits
#will be triggered. It works in conjunction with batch size. If batch
#size is greater than zero then if batch size is not reached but time
#interval is reached then commit will be triggered.
lucene.commit.time.interval=300000
```

Application Server configuration best practices

In *Chapter 1, Architectural Best Practices*, we talked about the reference architecture. We choose Tomcat as an Application Server for Liferay Portal. We can choose to use any supported Application Server with Liferay Portal. In this section, we will learn the Application Server configuration best practices. We will focus on the Tomcat server, which is a part of our reference architecture.

Database connection pool configuration

Liferay Portal uses the database connection pool to perform the database operation. It is very important to size the database connection pool carefully. If the database connection pool size is lower than what is needed, it will slow down the system. Application threads will be in waiting mode because of busy connections. Similarly, if the database connection pool is oversized, it will consume more resources of both the Application Server and the Database Server. By default, the database connection pool is configured using `portal-ext.properties`. Liferay Portal also supports the database connection pool configuration through the Application Server. Liferay Portal can access the Application Server level data source using JNDI. It is recommended to use the JNDI-based database connection pool configuration. Ideally, the database connection pool should be sized at 20-30 percent of the thread pool configuration. In other words if we configure the maximum size of the thread pool to 100, the database connection pool should be sized around 20 to 30. In *Chapter 2, Load Balancing and Clustering Best Practices*, we configured the Liferay Portal cluster. Let's learn how to configure the database connection pool as per the best practices. This is in continuation to the setup we have done in *Chapter 2, Load Balancing and Clustering Best Practices*.

1. Stop both the Liferay Portal nodes if they are already running.

2. Edit `portal-ext.properties` of both `liferay-node-01` and `liferay-node-02`. Comment the following database connection properties:

   ```
   jdbc.default.driverClassName=com.mysql.jdbc.Driver
   jdbc.default.url=jdbc:mysql://<MySQL Database Server IP>/lportal?useUnicode=true&characterEncoding=UTF-8&useFastDateParsing=false
   jdbc.default.username=<MySQL Database User Name>
   jdbc.default.password=<MySQL Password>
   ```

3. Now, add the following property in the same file:

   ```
   jdbc.default.jndi.name=jdbc/LiferayPool
   ```

4. Now, edit the `ROOT.xml` file located in `node-01\liferay-portal-6.1.1-ce-ga2\ tomcat-7.0.27\conf\Catalina\localhost` and add the following entry within the `<Context>` tag:

   ```
   <Resource
   auth="Container"
   description="Portal DB Connection"
   driverClass="com.mysql.jdbc.Driver"
   maxPoolSize="75"
   minPoolSize="10"
   acquireIncrement="5"
   name="jdbc/LiferayPool"
   user="<MySQL Database User Name>"
   password="<MySQL Password>"
   factory="org.apache.naming.factory.BeanFactory"
   type="com.mchange.v2.c3p0.ComboPooledDataSource"
   jdbcUrl="jdbc:mysql://<MySQL Database Server IP>:3306/lportal?useUnicode=true&amp;characterEncoding=UTF-8&amp;useFastDateParsing=false"/>
   ```

> Change the IP, username, and password with the appropriate IP, username, and password of the MySQL database server with which the `lportal` database is accessible.

5. Apply the same changes on `node-02` and then restart both the Liferay Portal nodes.

We changed the database connection properties in the Liferay Portal configuration to use the JNDI-based data source. We defined the data source in `ROOT.xml`. We used the `c3p0` type connection pool. It internally uses the `c3p0` connection pool library. We can also use other types of connection pools like DBCP or Tomcat. As per the given configuration, we defined the maximum connections to 75 and minimum connections to 10. Connections will be created in bunches of five. It is recommended to start with the given connection pool configuration and tune the same during load testing.

JVM configuration

The Java Virtual Machine configuration affects the performance of any Java-based application greatly. The key areas of JVM configuration include:

- Heap configuration
- Garbage Collector configuration

Both of these areas affect JVM performance a great deal. Let's learn Garbage Collection and Heap configuration best practices in terms of Liferay Portal.

Garbage Collection

Garbage Collection is a process which runs frequently within the JVM and destroys objects which are unused. Java provides different types of Garbage Collectors. We can choose one of them by providing the JVM arguments. Java 6 provides the following three types of Garbage Collectors:

- **Serial Collector**: This runs a single thread to perform the whole Garbage Collection activity
- **Parallel Collector**: This performs minor Garbage Collections in parallel and provides better performance
- **Concurrent Collector**: This garbage collector performs most of the stuff in parallel and so will have very little pause in the application because of Garbage Collection

It is recommended to use Concurrent Collector, which gives the best performance. Here are the recommended Garbage Collector configuration parameters:

```
-XX:+UseParNewGC -XX:+UseConcMarkSweepGC -XX:+CMSParallelRemarkEnabled
-XX:ParallelGCThreads=16 -XX:+CMSCompactWhenClearAllSoftRefs -XX
:CMSInitiatingOccupancyFraction=85 -XX:+CMSScavengeBeforeRemark
-XX:+CMSConcurrentMTEnabled -XX:ParallelCMSThreads=2
```

The preceding JVM options enable the Concurrent Garbage Collector. It configures to use 16 Parallel Garbage Collector threads. It is recommended to configure Parallel Garbage Collector threads equal to the number of CPU cores. For example, if the Liferay Portal server has two quad core CPUs, this parameter should be configured to 8. It also configures to use two **CMS (Concurrent Mark and Sweep)** threads. Garbage Collection is a very vast subject, and it is recommended to go through the following URL for more details:

http://www.oracle.com/technetwork/java/javase/gc-tuning-6-140523.html

The Java Heap configuration

Another important aspect that affects the performance of Java Virtual Machine is **Java Heap**. JVM divides Java Heap into multiple sections. These sections include:

- Eden space
- Survivor space
- Old or tenured space
- Permanent generation space
- Code cache

It is very important to configure these spaces carefully for better performance. JVM Heap can be configured using JVM arguments. Here is the recommended JVM Heap configuration for Liferay Portal installed on a server with less than 8 GB RAM:

```
-server -XX:NewSize=700m -XX:MaxNewSize=700m -Xms2048m -Xmx2048m
-XX:MaxPermSize=200m -XX:SurvivorRatio=6 -XX:TargetSurvivorRatio=90 -
XX:MaxTenuringThreshold=15
```

If the RAM of the server is greater than or equal to 8 GB, it is recommended to configure the Liferay Portal tomcat server with the following JVM parameters:

```
-server -d64 -XX:NewSize=3072m -XX:MaxNewSize=3072m -Xms6144m
-Xmx6144m -XX:PermSize=200m-XX:MaxPermSize=200m -XX:SurvivorRatio=6
-XX:TargetSurvivorRatio=90 -XX:MaxTenuringThreshold=0-
XX:+UseParNewGC -XX:ParallelGCThreads=16-XX:+UseConcMarkSweepGC
-XX:+CMSParallelRemarkEnabled -XX:+CMSCompactWhenClearAllSoftRefs
-XX:CMSInitiatingOccupancyFraction=85 -XX:+CMSScavengeBeforeRemark
```

```
-XX:+CMSConcurrentMTEnabled -XX:ParallelCMSThreads=2-
XX:+UseLargePages -XX:LargePageSizeInBytes=256m
-XX:+UseCompressedOops -XX:+DisableExplicitGC -XX:-UseBiasedLocking
-XX:+BindGCTaskThreadsToCPUs -XX:+UseFastAccessorMethods
```

> These JVM configuration settings are recommended by the Liferay Engineering team and published in the Liferay Deployment Checklist.

The given JVM configurations are initial configuration and these parameters should be tuned during the Load Testing phase. Liferay portal tomcat server includes `setEnv.sh` and `setEnv.bat` files where we can set these JVM arguments.

JSP engine configuration

Every J2EE application server uses a JSP engine to implement a JSP Specification. The Tomcat server uses the Jasper JSP engine to implement the JSP Specification. The Jasper JSP engine provides various configurations which can impact the performance of the server. Let's learn how to configure the JSP engine to get the best performance with Liferay Portal.

1. Stop both the Liferay Portal nodes if they are already running.
2. Edit `web.xml` located in the `node-01\liferay-portal-6.1.1-ce-ga2\tomcat-7.0.27\conf\` directory of `liferay-node-01` and change the `JspServlet` entry with the following line of code:

```xml
<servlet>
  <servlet-name>jsp</servlet-name>
  <servlet-class>org.apache.jasper.servlet.JspServlet</servlet-class>
  <init-param>
    <param-name>development</param-name>
    <param-value>false</param-value>
  </init-param>
  <init-param>
    <param-name>mappedFile</param-name>
    <param-value>false</param-value>
  </init-param>
  <init-param>
    <param-name>genStrAsCharArray</param-name>
    <param-value>true</param-value>
  </init-param>
  <load-on-startup>3</load-on-startup>
</servlet>
```

3. Apply the same changes to `web.xml` of `liferay-node-02`.
4. Start both the Liferay Portal nodes.

By default, Tomcat's JSP engine runs in the development mode. In the development mode, the JSP engine frequently polls the filesystem for changes. In the production environment, the frequency of JSP file changes is very low. Hence, JSP engine's development mode adds overhead on the server. We disabled the development mode by setting it to `false`. By default, the Jasper JSP engine converts the JSP file to the servlet in such a way that each line of JSP becomes a `print` statement. This feature helps in debugging issues but affects the performance of the server. We disabled this option by configuring the `false` value for the `mappedFile` parameter. If text strings in JSP are generated as character arrays, it can improve the performance. We enabled this by adding the `genStrAsCharArray` parameter.

Thread pool configuration

In *Chapter 2, Load Balancing and Clustering Best Practices*, we learned about the AJP connector of the Liferay Portal Tomcat server. We configured ports of the AJP connector. We configured the Apache Web Server to connect with the Liferay Portal Tomcat server using the AJP port. For every request, the Tomcat server creates a worker thread. The Tomcat server maintains a pool of worker threads for better performance. It is very important to configure this thread pool very carefully. If the thread pool is configured with a limited number of threads, requests will be queued up in a waiting state. If the thread pool is oversized, it will consume more server resources and ultimately affect the performance of the system. It is recommended to configure the initial thread pool configuration in the `server.xml` file as follows:

```
<Connector port="8019" maxHttpHeaderSize="8192"
maxThreads="50" minSpareThreads="50" maxSpareThreads="50"
enableLookups="false" acceptCount="100" redirectPort="8443"
protocol="AJP/1.3"
connectionTimeout="20000" disableUploadTimeout="true"
URIEncoding="UTF-8" />
```

In the preceding configuration, we have set the maximum number of threads in the thread pool to `50`. This is the initial configuration and during the load test we need to tune this value. We also configured the maximum allowed waiting requests if all the worker threads are occupied by using the `acceptCount` attribute. We also configured the connection timeout for worker threads.

> Please refer to the following URL for more details on connector attributes:
> `http://tomcat.apache.org/tomcat-7.0-doc/config/ajp.html`

Apache Web Server configuration best practices

In *Chapter 2, Load Balancing and Clustering Best Practices*, we configured the software load balancer using the Apache Web Server. We discussed that around 20 percent to 30 percent of the load of the system will be handled by the Apache Web Server. It is very important to follow performance best practices in Apache Web Server configuration to get the best performance. In this section, we will learn performance best practices related to the Apache Web Server configuration.

Static content delivery

In *Chapter 1, Architectural Best Practices*, we discussed about delivering static content using the Apache Web Server. Delivering static resources of the Liferay Portal through the Apache Web Server can improve the response time enormously. When static resources are delivered through the Apache Web Server, no Application Server overhead is added and ultimately, it improves the response time and performance. We learned how to configure the software load balancer using the `mod_jk` module of Apache Web Server in *Chapter 2, Load Balancing and Clustering Best Practices*. Let's learn how to extend this configuration and deliver static content directly through the Apache Web Server.

1. Stop both the Liferay Portal nodes if they are already running.
2. Copy the following content from `liferay-node-01` to the `<APACHE_HOME>/htdocs` directory of the Apache Web Server:
    - `node-01\liferay-portal-6.1.1-ce-ga2\ tomcat-7.0.27\webapps\ROOT\html`
    - `node-01\liferay-portal-6.1.1-ce-ga2\ tomcat-7.0.27\webapps\ROOT\layouttpl`
    - `node-01\liferay-portal-6.1.1-ce-ga2\ tomcat-7.0.27\webapps\ROOT\wap`
    - `node-01\liferay-portal-6.1.1-ce-ga2\ tomcat-7.0.27\webapps\*` (except the root directory)
3. Edit the `mod_jk.conf` file located in the `<APACHE_HOME>/conf` directory, and add the following line of code after the `JkMount /* loadblancer` line:

```
JkUnMount /*.js loadbalancer
JkUnMount /*.png loadbalancer
JkUnMount /*.jpg loadbalancer
JkUnMount /*.gif loadbalancer
JkUnMount /*.ico loadbalancer
JkUnMount /*.swf loadbalancer
```

4. Now restart both the Liferay Portal nodes one by one and then restart the Apache Web Server.

In the given steps, we copied all the content from the Liferay Portal node to the public directory of the Apache Web Server. We then disabled delivering static resources through the load balancer. That in turn delivers all unmounted static resources from the Apache Web Server's `htdocs` directory. CSS files are also static files. They can be served from the Apache Web Server. We intentionally did not configure the Apache Web Server to serve CSS files because Liferay Portal 6.1 CSS files can have dynamic code. Liferay Portal 6.1 uses the SASS framework to parse dynamic code of CSS files when they are requested. If you are using an earlier version of Liferay, we can also serve CSS files through the Apache Web Server.

If we configure static resource delivery through the Apache Web Server, we need to make sure that we synchronize static resources from the Liferay Portal node to the Apache Web Server after every deployment. It is recommended to make this process automatic by creating shell scripts.

One of the UI best practices is to reduce the number of HTTP requests for static resources. This can be done by merging static resources like JavaScript. Liferay provides a built-in feature that merges most common JavaScript files dynamically. Liferay defines the most common JavaScript files used by an unauthenticated user using the `javascript.barebone.files` property. Similarly, it defines the most common JavaScript files used by an authenticated user using the `javascript.everything.files` property. Liferay combines these JS files into one file and stores in the Application Server's `temp` directory. Each and every page loads either the **barebone** or **everything** JS bundle. They load these JS files by calling `everything.jsp` and `barebone.jsp`.

As Liferay combines lots of JS into one file, it will be useful if we can serve these large JS files directly through the Web Server. We can do that by performing the following steps:

1. Access `barebone.jsp` and `everything.jsp` from the browser and save them into the local system.

   > `barebone.jsp` can be accessed by using `http://<Apache Web Server IP>/html/js/barebone.jsp?minifierType=js&minifierBundleId=javascript.barebone.files` and `everything.jsp` can be accessed by using `http://<Apache Web Server IP>/html/js/everything.jsp?minifierType=js&minifierBundleId=javascript.everything.files`.

2. Now copy the downloaded `barebone.jsp` and `everything.jsp` to the `<APACHE_HOME>/htdocs /html/js/` directory.

3. Edit the `mod_jk.conf` file located in the `<APACHE_HOME>/conf` directory, and add the following line of code after the `JkMount /* loadblancer` line:

   ```
   JkUnMount /html/js/barebone.jsp loadbalancer
   JkUnMount /html/js/everything.jsp loadbalancer
   ```

4. Now restart the Apache Web Server.

In these steps, we placed the generated `barebone.jsp` and `everything.jsp` responses on the Apache Web Server in the same context path. We also configured the Apache Web Server to deliver `everything.jsp` and `barebone.jsp` directly from the Apache Web Server public directory. These two files are required to be synchronized whenever any of the JS listed in the `javascript.barebone.files` or `javascript.everything.files` property. Even if either of the two properties is changed in the `portal-ext.properties` file, it is required to copy the latest version of `everything.jsp` and `barebone.jsp` on the Apache Web Server.

GZip compression configuration

In the servlet filter configuration section, we talked about disabling the `GZip filter` of the Liferay Portal server to improve performance. We talked about taking care of GZip compression, although the Apache Web Server gives better performance. Most of the browsers support compressed resources. It will improve the network data transfer if we can compress the HTTP response before sending it to the browser. Browsers will then decompress the response before rendering.

GZip is a famous compression algorithm supported by almost all the browsers. The Apache Web Server can be configured to compress the HTTP response using the GZip compression algorithm. Let's learn this by applying it to our setup.

1. Add a new file, `mod_deflate.conf`, in the `<APACHE_HOME>/conf` directory, and add the following content to it:

   ```
   LoadModule deflate_module modules/mod_deflate.so
   SetOutputFilter DEFLATE
   SetEnvIfNoCase Request_URI \.(?:gif|jpe?g|png)$ no-gzip dont-vary
   SetEnvIfNoCase Request_URI \.(?:exe|t?gz|zip|bz2|sit|rar)$ no-gzip dont-vary
   ```

2. Now edit the `httpd.conf` file located in the `<APACHE_HOME>/conf` directory and add the following lines at the bottom:

   ```
   Include mod_deflate.conf
   ```

3. Now restart the Apache Web Server.

The Apache Web Server ships with a `mod_deflate` module, which can compress all the responses. In the preceding steps, we first enabled the `mod_deflate` module by adding the `LoadModule` statement. We then enabled the output filter to compress all the responses using the `mod_deflate` module. We also provided the configuration to skip some of the resources, such as GIF, JPEG, and so on because they are already in a compressed format. We should skip all such resources that are already in compressed format.

Cache header configuration

Every browser caches static resources in their cache. This cache is controlled by the `Cache-Control` request header attribute. It is a good idea to set a longer cache expiration period for static resources, so that the browser will download them only when they are removed from the browser cache on cache expiration. The Apache Web Server provides a way to configure cache expiration for any resource.

As we use the Apache Web Server in front of Liferay Portal, we can configure a `Cache-Control` attribute using the Apache Web Server. Let's learn how to configure `Cache-Control` using the Apache Web Server configuration.

1. Add a new file, `mod_expires.conf`, in the `<APACHE_HOME>/conf` directory, and add the following content to it:

   ```
   # Turn on Expires and set default to 0
   ExpiresActive On
   ExpiresDefault A0

   # Set up caching on media files for 1 year (forever?)
   <FilesMatch "\.(flv|ico|pdf|avi|mov|ppt|doc|mp3|wmv|wav)$">
   ExpiresDefault A29030400
   Header append Cache-Control "public"
   </FilesMatch>

   # Set up caching on media files for 1 week
   <FilesMatch "\.(gif|jpg|jpeg|png|swf)$">
   ExpiresDefault A604800
   Header append Cache-Control "public"
   </FilesMatch>

   # Set up 2 Hour caching on commonly updated files
   <FilesMatch "\.(xml|txt|html|js|css)$">
   ExpiresDefault A7200
   Header append Cache-Control "proxy-revalidate"
   </FilesMatch>

   # Force no caching for dynamic files
   <FilesMatch "\.(php|cgi|pl|htm)$">
   ```

```
ExpiresActive Off
Header set Cache-Control "private, no-cache, no-store, proxy-
revalidate, no-transform"
Header set Pragma "no-cache"
</FilesMatch>
```

2. Now edit the `httpd.conf` file located in the `<APACHE_HOME>/conf` directory and add the following line at the bottom:

   ```
   Include mod_expires.conf
   ```

3. Restart the Apache Web Server.

In the preceding steps, we did not include the `LoadModule` directive for the `mod_expire` module in the `mod_expires.conf` file because it is normally done in the default `httpd.conf` file. If we do not find the `LoadModule` directive for the `mod_expire` module in `httpd.conf`, we need to add the same in the `mod_expire.properties` file. We then configured cache expiration values for various types of resources. For example, we configured cache expiration to `1 week` for images. If the Portal is stable and we are not making frequent changes to the Portal, it is advisable to set the expiration period longer. So, it is advisable to review the expiration period according to the nature of the Portal.

Apache Web Server MPM configuration

Apache Web Server's multiprocessing module is responsible for accepting requests on the network port on the server. MPM is also responsible for dispatching requests to children for processing. In order to fine-tune the Apache Web Server, MPM must be configured correctly. The Apache Web Server ships with different MPM options. It is important to select the right MPM. Here is the list of different MPM options:

- **Prefork**: This is the MPM that runs in a non-threaded model. Each child process serves one request at a time.
- **Worker**: This MPM implements a multi-process, multi-threaded model.
- **Event**: This MPM is designed to handle highly concurrent access. This MPM is excremental in Apache 2.2.

For our solution, it is recommended to use the Worker MPM. Every MPM provides a way to configure the size of the processes or threads pool. It is very important to configure these parameters properly to get the best performance. Here is the sample configuration setting that needs to be added in `httpd.conf` of the Apache Web Server:

```
<IfModule worker.c>
ServerLimit 16
StartServers 2
```

```
MaxClients       150
MinSpareThreads   25
MaxSpareThreads   75
ThreadsPerChild   25
</IfModule>
```

> To know which MPM is used by the Apache Web Server, the following command can be used:
>
> **httpd -l**
>
> This command can be run on an Apache Web Server. It returns a list of modules in which the Apache binary is compiled. If we find `prefork.c` in the result, it means that the Apache Web Server is using the Prefork MPM.

In the preceding configuration, the most important configuration parameter is `MaxClients`. This parameter defines the maximum number of concurrent requests that can be handled by the Apache Web Server at a time. The `MaxClients` value must be configured lower than or equal to the `maxThreads` value of the Tomcat's AJP connector. If the value of the `MaxClients` parameter is higher than `maxThreads` of the AJP connector, it is possible that the Liferay Portal server hangs up or some requests are dropped off. The Worker MPM is a multi-threaded MPM. So, each process starts multiple threads. The `ThreadsPerChild` parameter configures the maximum number of threads that can run within one process. The `ServerLimit` parameter is used to limit the maximum number of process that can be started by the server. The value of the `ServerLimit` parameter must be higher than `MaxClients` or `ThreadsPerChild`. It is advisable to configure these values carefully with respect to the physical memory on the Apache Web Server. During the load test, these values should be tuned along with the Tomcat server's thread pool configuration.

Summary

In this chapter, we learned the configuration best practices to deploy a high performing Liferay-Portal-based solution. We learned how to tweak the Liferay Portal configuration to achieve the best performance. We also learned how to configure the Liferay Portal Application Server by applying best practices. We learned the recommended configurations for the Liferay Portal Application Server. We extended the Apache Web Server configuration from *Chapter 2, Load Balancing and Clustering Best Practices* by applying performance best practices. With this knowledge, we can easily fine-tune our Liferay-Portal-based solution.

In the next chapter, we will focus on caching best practices to further improve the performance of the solution. So let's gear up to get started on caching best practices.

4
Caching Best Practices

Caching is a technique that allows you to transparently store data in temporary storage, and serve all future requests directly from the temporary storage. With the use of caching, we can make the system enormously fast by reducing processing on the application server, the database server, and so on. In *Chapter 1*, *Architectural Best Practices*, we talked about the caching support in Liferay Portal. In the previous chapter, we learned various performance-related configuration best practices. Now, in this chapter we will focus on the best caching practices related to the Liferay Portal solution.

By the end of this chapter we will have learned

- How to customize the Ehcache configuration
- Ehcache configuration best practices
- How to implement the cache using Terracotta

Customizing the Ehcache configuration

In *Chapter 2*, *Load Balancing and Clustering Best Practices*, we learned about Ehcache replication best practices. We learned about multiple ways to configure Ehcache replication. In this section, we will learn how to provide custom Ehcache configuration to tune the cache according to the needs of the Portal solution using the following steps:

1. Stop both Liferay Portal nodes if they are running.
2. Locate the `portal-impl.jar` file in the `node-01\liferay-portal-6.1.1-ce-ga2\ tomcat-7.0.27\webapps\ROOT\WEB-INF\lib` directory of `liferay-node-01`. Copy the JAR file into some temporary directory.

3. Now, using the following command, extract /ehcache/liferay-single-vm.xml, /ehcache/liferay-multi-vm-clustered.xml, and /ehcache/hibernate-clustered.xml into the temporary directory:

   jar xf portal-impl.jarehcache/liferay-single-vm.xmlehcache/liferay-multi-vm-clustered.xmlehcache/hibernate-clustered.xml

4. The preceding command will create the ehcache directory and extract three XML files. Now rename the ehcache directory to custom-ehcache.

5. Copy the custom-ehcache directory to the node-01\liferay-portal-6.1.1-ce-ga2\ tomcat-7.0.27\webapps\ROOT\WEB-INF\classes\ directory of liferay-node-01.

6. Now add the following properties in the portal-ext.properties file on liferay-node-01:

   net.sf.ehcache.configurationResourceName=/custom-ehcache/hibernate-clustered.xml
   ehcache.single.vm.config.location=/custom-ehcache/liferay-single-vm.xml
   ehcache.multi.vm.config.location=/custom-ehcache/liferay-multi-vm-clustered.xml

7. Repeat steps 2 to 6 on liferay-node-02.

8. Now restart both the Liferay Portal nodes.

We copied the existing Ehcache configuration files into our custom folder, and then informed Liferay Portal to use them by providing properties in the portal-ext.properties file. Before we discuss the purpose of these Ehcache configuration files, it is important to recap some of the basics of the Ehcache framework.

The Ehcache framework uses a component called the **cache manager**, which controls the life cycle of cached objects. The cache manager contains multiple cache buckets and each cache bucket stores a list of objects. To identify specific objects within a cache bucket, the cache manager stores the objects in the form of a key-value pair.

The following diagram provides a better understanding of object storage within Ehcache. As shown in the diagram, the cache manager has multiple cache buckets. Each bucket is identified by a unique name. Within each cache bucket, we have multiple key-value pairs.

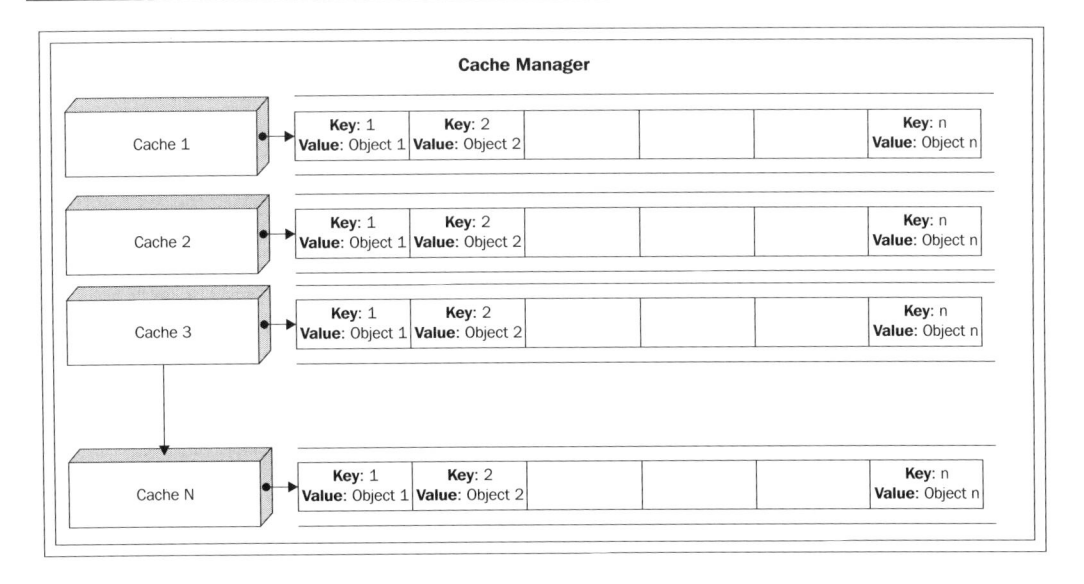

```
                        Cache Manager
  ┌─────────┐    ┌─────┬─────┬─────┬─────┬─────┐
  │ Cache 1 │────│Key:1│Key:2│     │     │Key:n│
  └─────────┘    │Val:O1│Val:O2│    │     │Val:On│
                 └─────┴─────┴─────┴─────┴─────┘
  ┌─────────┐    ┌─────┬─────┬─────┬─────┬─────┐
  │ Cache 2 │────│Key:1│Key:2│     │     │Key:n│
  └─────────┘    └─────┴─────┴─────┴─────┴─────┘
```

(Diagram: Cache Manager containing Cache 1, Cache 2, Cache 3, ... Cache N, each with Key/Value pairs.)

Ehcache provides a way to configure each cache bucket. This can be done by creating an XML configuration file and initializing the cache manager using the same XML configuration file. In this section, we extracted three different Ehcache XML configuration files. Internally, Liferay Portal defines three different cache managers using these configuration files. Let's learn the purpose of these cache managers.

Hibernate Ehcache CacheManager

Liferay uses the Hibernate framework for its persistence layer. The Hibernate framework supports two levels of caching:

- The first level of caching is implemented by the Hibernate framework itself
- The second level of caching is supported by external caching frameworks

In the default implementation, Liferay Portal uses the Ehcache framework for a second-level cache. Liferay includes a default Ehcache configuration file for a Hibernate-specific cache manager. It allows for providing a custom configuration file by adding the `net.sf.ehcache.configurationResourceName` property in `portal-ext.properties`. In the previous section, we extracted the `hibernate-clustered.xml` file from Liferay Portal and then configured Liferay to use this external file. In a clustered setup, this cache manager must be configured for cache replication.

Single-VM CacheManager

This cache manager is specifically used for caching those resources that do not require cache replication in a clustered environment. Such resources are static in nature, and it is OK to maintain a separate cache on each clustered node. One of the examples of such a resource is velocity templates associated with web content. Liferay Portal includes a default configuration file for this cache manager. In the previous section, we configured an external configuration file by adding the `ehcache.single.vm.config.location` property in the `portal-ext.properties` file.

Multi-VM CacheManager

This cache manager is used to cache those resources that are required to be replicated in a clustered setup. These resources include finder query responses, entities, service responses, and so on. These resources need to be cluster-aware, otherwise it will create functional issues. For example, consider a record of an entity cached on two Liferay Portal nodes. Now on one of the nodes, the same record is updated by specific functionality. The entity cache on the same node will be refreshed. If the cache for the same record on another Liferay node is not refreshed, users connected to that node will refer to an old record from the cache. Hence, the cache of such resources needs to be cluster-aware so that changes in the cache are reflected on all the nodes of a cluster. As this cache manager is cluster-aware, it is called a multi-VM pool. The Liferay bundle includes the default configuration file for this cache manager. Liferay Portal allows for providing a custom configuration file through the `ehcache.multi.vm.config.location` configuration property. In the previous section, we have a specified, external Ehcache configuration file by adding this property in `portal-ext.properties`.

Ehcache configuration best practices

We learned about the basics of Ehcache and also different cache managers used in Liferay Portal. Now let's focus on the cache manager configuration to tune the caching mechanism in Liferay. Using the cache manager configuration, we can provide a cache control parameter for each and every cache bucket. Let's understand the important configuration parameters by looking at the `defaultCache` and `cache` elements of the Liferay multi-VM cache manager configuration file.

```
<defaultCache
    eternal="false"
    maxElementsInMemory="10000"
    overflowToDisk="false"
    timeToIdleSeconds="600"
>
```

```
    <cacheEventListenerFactory
  class="com.liferay.portal.cache.ehcache.
LiferayCacheEventListenerFactory"
      properties="replicatePuts=false,replicateUpdatesViaCopy=false"
        propertySeparator=","
      />
      <bootstrapCacheLoaderFactory class="com.liferay.portal.cache.
  ehcache.LiferayBootstrapCacheLoaderFactory" />
    </defaultCache>
  <cacheeternal="false" maxElementsInMemory="10000"
    name="com.liferay.portlet.calendar.service.impl.CalEventLocalUtil"
      overflowToDisk="false"timeToIdleSeconds="600">
      <cacheEventListenerFactory
    class="com.liferay.portal.cache.ehcache.
LiferayCacheEventListenerFactory"
        properties="replicatePuts=false,replicateUpdatesViaCopy=false"
          propertySeparator=","/>
    <bootstrapCacheLoaderFactory class="com.liferay.portal.cache.ehcache.
LiferayBootstrapCacheLoaderFactory" />
  </cache>
```

As shown in the preceding code snippet, we have defined one cache bucket with a name `com.liferay.portlet.calendar.service.impl.CalEventLocalUtil`. This cache bucket stores the Calendar-portlet-related service responses in the cache. We have defined various cache control attributes in the `cache` tag. Some of the attributes are related to cache replication. Let's understand the important cache control attributes of the `cache` tag:

- `eternal`: This attribute indicates whether the objects placed in the specific cache can expire or not. If it is set to `true`, objects in the cache will never expire. It overrides the value of the `timeToIdleSeconds` attribute. We configured its value to `false` as we need to make sure cached objects are removed if they are not used.

- `maxElementsInMemory`: This attribute is important to size in-memory cache. It defines the maximum number of objects that can be stored in RAM. Once the number of objects in the cache bucket reaches this number, the cache manager removes the **least recently used** (**LRU**) object from the cache, if the `overflowToDisk` attribute is set to `false`.

- `timeToIdleSeconds`: This attribute defines the time for which an object can be in the cache without utilization. For example, the value of this parameter is set to 3600 for one of the cache buckets, and there is an object in the cache bucket which has not been accessed in the last hour. In this situation, such an object will be removed from the cache bucket. This attribute is also very important from the point of view of performance.

- **overflowToDisk**: This flag indicates whether to move cached objects to the filesystem when the number of objects in-memory exceeds the limit. Internally, the cache manager uses serialization and deserialization to read and write objects on the filesystem.

It is not mandatory to define a cache bucket in the configuration file. The Ehcache framework also allows for creating new cache buckets programmatically. In that situation, a cache bucket is created with the default cache control attributes. The default cache control attributes are provided by the defaultCache element in the configuration file. In the previous snippet, we have set the same cache control attributes in the defaultCache element.

We learned about the importance and use of cache control attributes. Let's talk about the best practices associated with them:

- It is recommended to disable the overflowToDisk attribute. If it is enabled, it will generate more IO and will ultimately affect the performance. If the system is expected to have a huge amount of cache, it is a good idea to choose a centralized cache such as Terracotta rather than enabling the overflowToDisk attribute.

- It is recommended to set the eternal attribute to false. It is fine to enable this attribute when the number of elements in the cache bucket is low and they are accessed frequently by the Portal.

- It is recommended to configure the maxElementsInMemory attribute as per the application need. It has to be calculated properly based on the application need. If the value is low, cache objects are removed frequently from the cache.

- Depending upon the application need, timeToIdleSeconds should be properly configured for every cache bucket. If the value is too low, cache objects are frequently removed from the cache. Similarly, if the value is high, the system will occupy memory for unused cached objects.

As there are so many cache buckets to tune cache control parameters, we need to first decide which cache buckets are of our interest. This can be decided based on the kind of features that we are using. For example, Portal heavily uses collaboration features. In that situation, some of the important cache buckets could be as follows:

```
com.liferay.portal.kernel.dao.orm.EntityCache.com.liferay.portlet.
blogs.model.impl.BlogsEntryImpl
com.liferay.portal.kernel.dao.orm.EntityCache.com.liferay.portlet.
wiki.model.impl.WikiPageImpl
com.liferay.portal.kernel.dao.orm.EntityCache.com.liferay.portlet.
messageboards.model.impl.MBCategoryImpl
com.liferay.portal.kernel.dao.orm.EntityCache.com.liferay.portlet.
messageboards.model.impl.MBThreadImpl
```

It is difficult to calculate cache control parameters for all cache buckets in the beginning. Hence, it is recommended to tune them during the load-testing phase. During the load-testing phase, we should monitor cache statistics and then the cache control parameters should be tuned based on the cache statistics result.

Caching using Terracotta

In *Chapter 1, Architectural Best Practices*, we talked about various caching options for our Liferay-based solution. We discussed using Terracotta as a centralized cache server. If the portal is designed to handle huge amounts of traffic and transactions, it will need a good amount of cache to provide the best performance. In such situations, it is recommended to go with a high-end, centralized cache server. Terracotta is one of the most popular products in this space. We can configure Liferay Portal to cache resources in Terracotta instead of in embedded Ehcache. Let's learn how to configure Liferay Portal to cache resources in a Terracotta server. We will configure Terracotta-based caching for our clustered setup using the following steps:

1. Download and install Terracotta in a directory on a separate server. This directory is referred to as TERRACOTTA_HOME.

   > The Terracotta community edition can be downloaded from http://terracotta.org/downloads/open-source/catalog. We need to download terracotta-x.x.x-installer.jar. Here, x.x.x is the version of the Terracotta community edition. We need to follow the installation steps mentioned at the site to install the Terracotta server.

2. Now stop the two Liferay Portal servers if they are running.

3. Locate the node-01\liferay-portal-6.1.1-ce-ga2\ tomcat-7.0.27\webapps\ROOT\WEB-INF\lib directory on liferay-node-01 and remove the following files:

   ehcache*.jar
   slf4j*.jar

4. Locate the TERRACOTTA_HOME\ehcache\lib\ directory on the Terracotta server and copy the following JAR files to the node-01\liferay-portal-6.1.1-ce-ga2\ tomcat-7.0.27\webapps\ROOT\WEB-INF\lib directory on liferay-node-01:

   ehcache*.jar
   slf4j*.jar

5. Locate the `$TERRACOTTA_HOME\common` directory and copy the following JAR file to the `node-01\liferay-portal-6.1.1-ce-ga2\ tomcat-7.0.27\ webapps\ROOT\WEB-INF\lib` directory:

   terracotta-toolkit*.jar

6. Create the `terracotta-cache` directory in the `node-01\liferay-portal-6.1.1-ce-ga2\ tomcat-7.0.27\webapps\ROOT\WEB-INF\classes\` directory and create the `hibernate-terracotta.xml` file with following content:

```
<ehcache
  dynamicConfig="false"
  name="hibernate-terracotta"
  updateCheck="false"
  xmlns:xsi="http://www.w3.org/2001/XMLSchema-instance"
  xsi:noNamespaceSchemaLocation="ehcache.xsd"
>
  <defaultCache
    eternal="false"
    maxElementsInMemory="100000"
    overflowToDisk="false"
    timeToIdleSeconds="600"
  >
    <terracotta />
  </defaultCache>
  <cache
    eternal="false"
    maxElementsInMemory="100000"
    name="com.liferay.portal.model.impl.UserImpl"
    overflowToDisk="false"
    timeToIdleSeconds="600"
  >
    <terracotta />
  </cache>
<terracottaConfig url="<IP/host name of Terracotta
Server>:<terracotta server port>" />
</ehcache>
```

> Change the host name and port in the `terracottaConfig` tag accordingly.

7. Create the `liferay-multi-vm-terracotta.xml` file in the `node-01\liferay-portal-6.1.1-ce-ga2\ tomcat-7.0.27\webapps\ROOT\WEB-INF\classes\terracotta-cache` directory with the following content:

   ```
   <ehcache
     dynamicConfig="false"
     name="liferay-multi-vm-terracotta"
     updateCheck="false"
     xmlns:xsi="http://www.w3.org/2001/XMLSchema-instance"
     xsi:noNamespaceSchemaLocation="ehcache.xsd">
   <defaultCache
     eternal="false"
     maxElementsInMemory="10000"
     overflowToDisk="false"
     timeToIdleSeconds="600">
     <terracotta />
   </defaultCache>
   <cache
     eternal="false"
     maxElementsInMemory="10000"
   name="com.liferay.portlet.journalcontent.util.JournalContent"
     overflowToDisk="false"
     timeToIdleSeconds="600">
     <terracotta />
   </cache>
   <terracottaConfig url="<IP/host name of Terracotta Server>:<terracotta server port>" />
   </ehcache>
   ```

8. Add the following properties in `portal-ext.properties` of the `liferay-node-01` file to enable Terracotta-based caching:

   ```
   net.sf.ehcache.configurationResourceName=/terracotta-cache/hibernate-terracotta.xml
   ehcache.multi.vm.config.location=/terracotta-cache/liferay-multi-vm-terracotta.xml
   hibernate.cache.region.factory_class=net.sf.ehcache.hibernate.SingletonEhCacheRegionFactory
   ```

9. Repeat steps 3 to 8 on `liferay-node-02` and restart the Terracotta server and both Liferay Portal nodes.

Terracotta internally uses the Ehcache framework for caching. Hence, we replaced the Ehcache-related JAR files from the Terracotta installation. We then created the cache manager configuration file for the Hibernate cache manager and multi-VM cache manager. These XML files look similar to the Ehcache configuration files. In addition to the cache bucket configuration, we also provided Terracotta server details in the file. Within every cache bucket entry, we added the `terracotta` tag to inform the cache manager to store cached objects in the Terracotta server.

In the Terracotta configuration files, we configured only one cache bucket. For all other buckets, it will use cache control attributes of the `defaultCache` element. It is recommended to configure all the important cache buckets by adding cache entry in these configuration files. As it uses the same Ehcache XML schema, we can optimize each cache bucket by providing the same cache control attributes that we learned about in the previous section. Unlike Ehcache-based cache implementation, Terracotta provides a GUI-based tool called **Developer Console** for monitoring and diagnosis. This tool is useful to monitor cache buckets during the load test.

We used Terracotta only for caching resources but it also provides a way to store HTTP sessions and Quartz jobs in it. It is recommended to configure Liferay Portal to store HTTP sessions and Quartz jobs on Terracotta if we are using Terracotta for caching. This will reduce the overhead of replication.

Summary

In this chapter, we learned the best caching practices of Liferay Portal. We learned how to configure the default Ehcache-based caching mechanism to achieve better performance. We learned the different types of caches in Liferay Portal. We also learned about advance caching implementation using Terracotta. With this knowledge, we can improve the performance of our Liferay Portal-based solution by optimizing the caching mechanism.

So far we learned the architectural best practices, load balancing, and clustering best practices, configuration best practices, and caching best practices.

Now it's time to gear up for development best practices.

Development Best Practices

5

In the previous chapters, we learned about various configuration best practices including caching best practices. Liferay Portal is a portal platform, and portal solutions are developed on top of it. Hence, it is very important to follow best practices during the development of custom features to build high performing portal solutions. In this chapter, we will focus on Liferay-Portal-specific development best practices. By the end of this chapter, we will learn the following topics:

- UI best practices
    - Reducing the number of JavaScript files
    - Reducing the number of CSS files
    - Using CSS image sprites
    - Minifying JavaScript files
    - JavaScript tag positioning
    - Analyzing web page performance using tools
- Java development best practices
    - Use of dynamic query and custom queries
    - Use of the Cache API to cache resources
    - Coding best practices

UI best practices

In any web-based applications, loading and rendering of the user interface in the browser contributes a lot in overall response time. It can even sometimes affect the processing on the server. In this section, we will talk about various UI best practices for improving the performance of the Portal.

Reducing the number of JavaScript files

JavaScript files are an integral part of web pages. There are two ways to include JavaScript in an HTML response:

- One way is to embed JavaScript directly in the response using the `<script>` tag
- The second is by referring to an independent JavaScript file using the `<script>` tag

It is recommended to include JavaScript using the second option. This allows the browser to cache JavaScript files separately in the browser cache. With the use of powerful JavaScript frameworks such as jQuery, YUI, Alloy UI, and so on, it is possible that one HTML page might be loading many different JavaScript files. This can slow down loading of the page in the browser because of network transfer. Transferring a number of small files over the network takes more time than transferring a single large file. Hence, it is recommended to reduce the number of JavaScript files by merging them together before transferring them over the network. This technique can improve the overall response time of the system.

Liferay Portal by default includes a lot of JavaScript files to implement various features. These files are required by either Portal's core features or by bundled portlets. If these JavaScript files are merged into a single JavaScript before transferring over the network, it can improve the overall performance of the Portal. This can be done by statically merging them but it will affect the maintenance of these files. For this reason, Liferay Portal has implemented a feature with which it dynamically combines these JavaScript files. Liferay Portal loads the combined JavaScript at once to improve the response time.

This feature can be enabled by adding the following property in the `portal-ext.properties` file:

```
javascript.fast.load=true
```

This property is by default configured to `true`, but sometimes developers set this property to `false` to debug JavaScript issues. The same configuration may be replicated in the production environment by mistake. Hence, it is very important to make sure this property is enabled in the production environment. When this property is enabled, Liferay Portal dynamically merges the list of JavaScript files. This list is known as the **JavaScript bundle**. Liferay Portal by default defines two bundles:

- The barebone bundle
- The everything bundle

When the Portal is accessed without authentication, every portal request loads the barebone bundle in the response. If the user accesses the Portal after authentication, every portal request loads the everything bundle in the response. Liferay Portal configures these JavaScript bundles using the configuration property. We can modify the list of files that are loaded by these bundles. The content of the barebone bundle can be modified by adding the following property in the `portal-ext.properties` file:

```
javascript.barebone.files=
```

In this property, we need to provide comma-separated JavaScript files. We can provide a relative path of the JavaScript files from the `/html/js` directory of the ROOT web application. For example, suppose we are using an AUI-based dialog box on most of our pages. It will require loading the `aui-dialog.js` file located in the `liferay-portal-6.1.20-ee-ga2\tomcat-7.0.27\webapps\ROOT\html\js\aui\aui-dialog\` directory. Instead of making a separate request for this file from the browser, we can add this file in the barebone bundle. This can be done by appending `aui\aui-dialog\ aui-dialog.js` to the existing values of the `javascript.barebone.files` property in `portal-ext.properties`.

To configure the list of JavaScript files of the everything bundle, we need to add the following property in `portal-ext.properties`:

```
javascript.everything.files=
```

By default, the everything bundle extends the barebone bundle. So, in the everything bundle, we need to provide only those JavaScript files that are not there in the barebone bundle. Liferay also provides a way to disable the barebone bundle. If we disable the barebone bundle, Liferay Portal loads the everything bundle for both authenticated and nonauthenticated requests. We can disable the barebone bundle by adding the following property in the `portal-ext.properties` file:

```
javascript.barebone.enabled=false
```

So far we talked about merging the JavaScript files of the Liferay Portal bundle. But we use Liferay Portal as a platform and develop portlets on top of it. Portlets also contain JavaScript files. It is recommended to merge the commonly-used JavaScript files of a portlet into one portlet to reduce the number of JavaScript requests.

> The JavaScript merging feature of Liferay is implemented using the `minifier` filter. Hence, it is very important to make sure the `minifier` filer is not disabled. The `minifier` filter is by default enabled but can be controlled by using the following property:
>
> ```
> com.liferay.portal.servlet.filters.minifier.MinifierFilter
> ```

Reducing the number of CSS files

Similar to JavaScript files, CSS files are also an integral part of every web page, and a web page can have many CSS files loaded through the `link` tag. Again, inline styles through the `<style>` tag are not recommended. Similar to JavaScript merging, CSS files can also be merged to reduce network overhead. Liferay provides configuration to automatically merge CSS files of themes. This can be done by enabling the following property in `portal-ext.properties`:

```
theme.css.fast.load=true
```

If this property is enabled, it will always merge all the CSS files into one and load the merged CSS files on every page. By default this property is enabled by Liferay Portal. During development it may be required to disable this property to solve CSS-related issues. But in the production environment, this property should be set to `true` to get the best performance.

This feature only covers theme-related CSS files. We can also have CSS files in portlets. It is recommended to merge CSS files of the portlets into a single CSS file.

Using CSS image sprites

We looked at reducing the number of JavaScript and CSS file requests by merging them into a single file. Similar to that, every web page will have many network requests for images. Unlike CSS and JavaScript files, images are a different kind of resource and they need to be placed on the HTML page at a certain location. Hence, it is not possible to simply merge them, unlike CSS and JavaScript files, to reduce network overhead. To reduce the number of image requests, a technique called **CSS image sprites** is used. CSS image sprites are a pure HTML-and-CSS-based technique. Liferay provides built-in support for CSS image sprites through its tag libraries. Before we talk about Liferay Portal's CSS image sprites capability, let's understand how CSS image sprites work.

Suppose we have a simple HTML response with multiple static images as follows:

```
<html>
  <body>
    Arrow Up : <img src='arrow_up.png' />
    Arrow Down : <img src='arrow_down.png' />
    Arrow Right : <img src='arrow_right.png' />
    Arrow Left : <img src='arrow_left.png' />
  </body>
</html>
```

As shown in this code snippet, we are loading four images in the browser. To reduce the number of image requests, we need to combine all four images as shown:

Now the next step is to change the HTML code to render individual images from the preceding combined image:

```html
<html>
  <body>
    Arrow Up : <img src='spacer.png' width='16px' height='16px' style='background:url(arrow_sprite.png) 0 48;' />
    Arrow Down : <img src='spacer.png' width='16px' height='16px' style='background:url(arrow_sprite.png) 0 0;' />
    Arrow Right : <img src='spacer.png' width='16px' height='16px' style='background:url(arrow_sprite.png) 0 32;'/>
    Arrow Left : <img src='spacer.png' width='16px' height='16px' style='background:url(arrow_sprite.png) 0 16;'/>
  </body>
</html>
```

This means we are now using one large image to load four different images. This concept is called CSS image sprites. The combined image is called a **sprite image**.

This technique is very good but it requires a lot of development effort. In the case of Portal, we need to create many image sprites for portlets, themes, and so on. We also need to add a lot of CSS styles to use sprite images. Fortunately, Liferay Portal provides built-in support for CSS image sprites. The Liferay plugin deployer automatically generates sprite images by combining all the images in one folder. Along with that it also generates a file called _sprites.properties. This file stores the size and coordinates of each image. Liferay tag libraries internally read this information and automatically generate the image tags to load the specific image from the sprite image.

Let's assume, in our custom theme, that we included the previous four images in the images\arrows folder. Now when we deploy the theme on Liferay Portal, it generates the _sprite.png, _sprite.gif, and _sprite.properties files in the same folder. Both of the images will look similar to the image shown in this section. The content of the _sprite.properties file will look as follows:

```
/arrows/01_down.png=0,16,16
/arrows/01_left.png=16,16,16
/arrows/01_right.png=32,16,16
/arrows/01_up.png=48,16,16
```

As shown in the preceding snippet, the property file defines a key-value kind of structure. The key is the name of the individual image file. The value contains the width, height, and top *y* coordinate of the individual image in pixels. Liferay tag libraries take image names as an input. With the use of this property file, they can load individual images from `_sprite.png`. As mentioned earlier, Liferay Portal also generates `_sprite.gif`, which is used for old browsers.

This feature of Liferay Portal can be easily disabled or enabled. By default this feature is enabled. During the development phase, developers may want to disable this feature. It can be disabled by adding the following property in `portal-ext.properties`:

```
theme.images.fast.load=false
```

It is recommended to keep this property set to `true` in the production environment.

We looked at how CSS image sprites work for built-in features. We can also use Liferay tag libraries in custom portlets to load images from a theme. To load an image from an image sprite, we can simple use the `icon` tag of the `liferay-ui` tag library. Here is an example code snippet from a custom portlet that is loading an image from a theme:

```
<%@ taglib uri="http://liferay.com/tld/theme" prefix="liferay-theme"
%>
<liferay-ui:icon src='<%= themeDisplay.getTheme().
getContextPath()+"/"+ themeDisplay.getTheme().getImagesPath() + "/
common/activate.png" %>' />
```

As shown in the preceding code snippet, we loaded an image from the theme. We just provided the path of the image. Internally, depending upon the value of the `theme.images.fast.load` property, Liferay loads the individual image or sprite image.

Minifying JavaScript files

Minification is a technique to reduce the number of characters from JavaScript files without affecting the functionality. With this technique, we can reduce the size of JavaScript files and improve the response time. It is recommended to use minified JavaScript files in the production environment.

Once JavaScript files are minified, it becomes difficult to read, debug, or modify them. Hence, it is a best practice to keep both minified and nonminified files in a version control system. In the production environment, only the minified version of JavaScript files should be deployed. In order to make sure all the JavaScript files are minified, it is recommended to automate the minification of the files through build scripts. This can be easily done by adding a target in an ANT build script.

> To minify JavaScript files of a specific plugin of the Liferay plugin SDK automatically, we need to add an ANT task in the `build.xml` file of the plugin. From the ANT task, we need to call minifier to minify all JavaScript files of the plugin. YUI Compressor is one of the most popular open source JavaScript minifiers. It can be called from the ANT task. The following URL provides more details on how to call the YUI Compressor from an ANT task:
>
> https://code.google.com/p/yui-compressor-ant-task/

JavaScript positioning

As per the HTTP/1.1 specification, the browser should not download more than two resources per host name. But with JavaScript files, this rule works differently. When the browser is downloading JavaScript, it blocks all other download requests irrespective of the host name. This affects the overall response time. The Yahoo! team found out that if JavaScript files are placed outside of the html tag, this problem can be avoided and pages load faster. Here is an example code from `yahoo.com`:

```
</html>
<!-- dnr= -->
<!-- bid=704 -->
<!-- sid=97684142 -->
<!-- myproperty:myservice-in:0:Success -->
<script language=javascript>
if(window.yzq_p==null)document.write("<scr"+"ipt language=javascript src=http://l.yimg.com/d/lib/bc/bcr_2.0.5.js></scr"+"ipt>");
</script>
```

As shown here, the `<script>` tag is placed after the end of the `<html>` tag. This is against the specification but all browsers support it. Hence, it is recommended to place JavaScript files outside the `<html>` tag in the footer. It is not possible to place all JavaScript files in the footer but whenever possible, we should place the files like this.

This is a good technique but in case of Portal, we develop portlets and they do not have `<html>` or `<body>` tags. They just render HTML fragments. Fortunately, Liferay provides a way to add JavaScript files in the page footer from any portlet. This can be done by providing the `<footer-portal-javascript>` tag in `liferay-portlet.xml` as shown:

```
<footer-portlet-javascript>/html/portlet/users_admin/js/main.js</footer-portlet-javascript>
```

Limiting the use of DOM operations

Document Object Model (DOM) is a convention for representing HTML objects. With the use of DOM operations, we can change the state of HTML objects displayed on the browser. With DOM, it will be very easy to programmatically manipulate HTML content rendered on the browsers. Frameworks such as jQuery, AUI, or YUI reduces the amount of code required to perform DOM operations. DOM operations are browser-dependent. Each browser provides its own implementation for DOM. Some of the browsers such as IE7 or IE8 are not optimized to perform DOM operations. DOM operations slow down the rendering of web pages in the browser. It is recommended to use fewer DOM operations in the code to make the system run faster.

Analyzing web page performance using tools

In this section, we talked about some of the key UI best practices. UI is a very vast field and there are many such best practices. These best practices can be applied to any web-based applications. It is very difficult to find out areas of the UI where we are not following such best practices. Fortunately, there are many tools available to find out improvement areas from the UI point of view. Here are some of the more popular tools, which we can use to find out areas of improvements:

- **YSlow**: YSlow is an open source tool to point out issues that can affect the performance of the system. It checks the web page against around 23 rules. Based on the result it gives a performance grade. It can be installed as a browser plugin. It supports most of the popular browsers. For more information please refer to `http://yslow.org/`.

- **PageSpeed**: This is another web page analysis tool to point out bad practices. It checks the pages against web page performance best practices. It is open source and can be used as a browser plugin. It can also be configured on Apache Web Server. For more information please refer to `https://developers.google.com/speed/pagespeed/https://developers.google.com/speed/pagespeed/`.

- **Compuware dynaTrace AJAX Edition**: This tool installs an application agent in the browser. With that it can record all requests. Based on the analysis it points out areas of improvement. It also gives a performance grade to each page. This tool persists performance reports and so it makes it easy to compare the results after applying changes. For more information please refer to `http://www.compuware.com/application-performance-management/ajax-performance-testing.html`.

There are many other tools available in the market but I have listed out some of the key tools based on my experience.

Portlet development best practices

We talked about some of the key UI best practices. Now let's talk about some of the key portlet development best practices to achieve best performance.

Limiting the use of dynamic queries

To implement the service and persistence layer in custom portlets, Liferay provides a very good code generator called **Service Builder**. Service Builder generates a persistence layer using the Hibernate framework. Service Builder also generates code in the Service and Persistence classes to cache responses in a multi-VM cache pool. Service Builder provides a way to define finder methods using an XML configuration. Responses of these finder methods are also cached in a multi-VM cache pool. Liferay Service Builder also provides a way to execute dynamic queries using the dynamic query API. Service Builder generates methods in the service and persistence layer to execute dynamic queries. Here is an example of dynamic query execution:

```
DynamicQuery query = DynamicQueryFactoryUtil.forClass(CalEvent.class)
.add(PropertyFactoryUtil.forName("groupId").in(new Long[]
{new Long(1L),new Long(2L)})) .add(PropertyFactoryUtil.
forName("startDate").ge(CalendarFactoryUtil.getCalendar().getTime())).
addOrder(OrderFactoryUtil.asc("startDate"));
List events2 = CalEventLocalServiceUtil.dynamicQuery(query);
```

As shown in the preceding code snippet, a dynamic query makes it easy to query the database without creating the specific finder. But unlike regular finder methods, Liferay does not generate code to cache dynamic query responses. To cache a query response, Liferay needs a unique cache key. For regular finder methods, the key is generated from method arguments. But for a dynamic query, it will be difficult to generate a unique key from arguments. Also it will be difficult to implement cache invalidation logic for dynamic queries.

It is recommended to limit the use of dynamic queries because they are not cached. They increase the load on the database server and ultimately affect the performance of the system. They can be used along with a custom caching implementation.

Liferay caching API

In *Chapter 4, Caching Best Practices*, we discussed Liferay's caching capabilities in detail. We talked about different cache pools used by Liferay Portal. We talked about the cluster-enabled multi-VM cache pool and nonclustered single-VM cache pool. Liferay provides an API to add custom cache buckets in both cache pools. This API can be used by custom portlets or plugins for caching. By using Liferay's caching APIs, we can leverage Liferay's built-in cache support. We do not need to worry about cache replication, cache monitoring, or cache configuration. They are handled at the portal level.

To use Liferay's caching API, first we need to decide which cache pool we want to use. As discussed in *Chapter 4, Caching Best Practices*, a single-VM cache pool is ideal for resources that are unique per node and do not require cache replication. Here is an example class from a custom portlet that utilizes a single-VM pool:

```java
package com.connectsam.development;

import com.liferay.portal.kernel.cache.SingleVMPoolUtil;
import java.util.ArrayList;
import java.util.List;

public class SingleVMPoolExample {
    public List<String> getTestList(String key){
      List<String> listOfStrings = null;
//Retrieve List from Single-VM Pool by passing Cache Name and Key of cached object
listOfStrings = (List<String>) SingleVMPoolUtil.get("com.connectsam.development.SingleVMPoolExample",key);
        if(listOfStrings == null){
//If object not found in cache then retrieve the object from source
          listOfStrings = getSampleList();
          //Put the retrieved object in cache
SingleVMPoolUtil.put( "com.connectsam.development.SingleVMPoolExample",key, listOfStrings);
        }
        return listOfStrings;
    }
    private List<String> getSampleList(){
      List<String> list = new ArrayList<String>();
      list.add("Single VM List");
      return list;
    }
}
```

As shown in the preceding code snippet, we used the `SingleVMPoolUtil` class to store objects in the cache. It is recommended to define the Utility class within the custom portlet for handling cache-related functions. To use the multi-VM cache pool, we can use the exact same approach as previously mentioned. Instead of using `SingleVMPoolUtil`, we will need to use the `MultiVMPoolUtil` class to store and retrieve objects from the cache. As discussed in *Chapter 4, Caching Best Practices*, a multi-VM cache pool should be used for caching those resources that require cache replication across the cluster.

Coding best practices

We briefly talked about some of the key Liferay-Portal-specific best practices. But it is proven that most of the time performance issues arise from poorly-written code. For example, if database connections are not properly closed, even caching will not improve the performance. It is recommended to use standard automated code analysis tools to find out coding violations. Automated code analysis tools help us to locate performance-specific violations such as open JDBC connections, unused variables, and so on. Here are some of the popular code analysis tools:

- PMD
- CPD
- FindBugs
- SONAR

It is also required to perform manual code reviews to point out low-level design issues.

Summary

We learned various performance-specific UI and portlet development best practices. We learned how to use Liferay Portal's JavaScript bundle mechanism to reduce the number of JavaScript requests. We learned how to reduce the number of image requests using CSS image sprites. We learned how to use Liferay Portal's cache API to cache objects in custom portlets. We also learned about automated code analysis and web page analysis tools to point out performance issues. With this knowledge, we can ensure we develop the best performing code during the development phase.

Now let's gear up to learn about load testing and tuning Liferay-based systems.

6
Load Testing and Performance Tuning

In *Chapter 5*, *Development Best Practices*, we learned about performance-related development best practices. Throughout the book, we learned many best practices to improve the performance of Liferay-Portal-based solutions. Even after applying those best practices, it is very important to verify whether the system meets performance expectations under the anticipated peak load. This can be done by performing load testing. We also talked about many dynamic configurations as well, which can be further tuned during load testing to meet performance expectations. In this chapter, we will learn load testing and performance tuning best practices for a Liferay-Portal-based solution.

In this chapter, we will cover the following topics:

- Getting ready for load testing
    - Capturing load testing requirements
    - Selecting a load testing tool
    - Writing load testing scripts
    - Setting up the load testing environment
    - Conducting load tests
- Resource monitoring and performance tuning
    - Liferay Portal server – monitoring and tuning
    - Apache web server – monitoring and tuning
    - Monitoring the database server
    - Monitoring logfiles

Getting ready for load testing

Load testing is an exercise to validate the system's capability to handle expected peak load. The maximum number of concurrent requests that the system is expected to handle is known as the **peak load**. Load testing is performed by artificially generating a number of concurrent requests on the system using load testing tools. To begin with the load testing exercise, the first step would be to capture that load testing requirements.

Capturing load testing requirements

To perform load testing, we need to design load testing scenarios, set up load testing environments, and so on. Load testing scenarios heavily depend on load testing or performance-related requirements. Also, depending on the performance requirements, a load testing environment has to be set up. Here is a brief checklist to capture all load-testing-related requirements:

1. **Concurrent users**: It is very important to know the maximum amount of load that is expected on the system. It is measured by the number of users accessing the system at the same time. This is the most important requirement to be captured to conduct load testing. Sometimes concurrent user requirements are more specific, such as X number of concurrent users who will access page Y. If such requirements are available, load testing scenarios can be designed realistically. This requirement acts as an input for a load testing exercise.

2. **Response time**: It is also very important to measure the response time of every request when the system is heavily loaded. Every system has accepted the response time limit. Here is some examples of response time requirements:

    - The response time for all pages except the home page should be less than or equal to 4 seconds. The home page response time should be less than or equal to 8 seconds.
    - It is impossible to make sure that the response time of all requests stays within the expected limits. Hence, most of the time the response time is referred to as the average response time. Sometimes requirements specifically state that an X percentage of requests must have a response time in the given range. It is very important to capture such details to design load testing scenarios and acceptance criteria accordingly. Response time requirement acts as an acceptance criteria for the load testing exercise.

3. **Transactions per second (throughput)**: In transaction centric portals, it is important to measure the number of transactions executed per second. This is called **TPS** or **throughput**. It is very important to capture the expected throughput under pick load. Again, throughput-related requirements act as acceptance criteria for the load testing exercise.

Selecting load testing tools

Load testing requires generating artificial user requests. This can be done by load testing tools. There are many proprietary and open source load testing tools available in the market. It is very important to choose the right tool for the load testing exercise. In this section, we will briefly talk about some of the open source or cloud-based load testing tools.

Apache JMeter

Apache JMeter is the most popular open source tool for conducting load testing. It is shipped as a desktop application and provides a user-friendly GUI for creating load testing scripts. Apache JMeter is highly extensible and supports external plugins. It comes with many built-in plugins. It has many plugins to generate user-friendly output reports. It also comes up with many plugins that allow the exporting of load testing reports to various formats such as CSV, XLS, and so on. Apache JMeter supports load testing of the following type of requests:

- HTTP or HTTPS
- SOAP
- LDAP
- JMS
- Database via JDBC
- SMTP, POP3, or IMAP
- Shell scripts

BlazeMeter

BlazeMeter is a cloud-based load testing tool. Internally, it runs a cluster of JMeter instances. Hence, it supports generating a huge amount of load. Similar to JMeter, it supports similar types of requests. It provides good interactive reporting. It supports generating load from different geographic locations to perform realistic load tests. It also supports scheduling load tests.

Apache Benchmark (ab)

Apache Benchmark is a command-line load testing tool to perform simple load tests for HTTP requests. It uses a single operating system thread for generating load. Hence, it is not advisable to use it for a large number of concurrent requests. It generates load on the server by requesting the given URL concurrently. It does not download subsequent resources such as CSS, JS, Images, and so on. It does not provide user-friendly reporting as well. Also, it doesn't support testing multiple URLs at the same time.

Other than these three tools, there are many popular and powerful proprietary tools available in the market. Some of the popular tools include HP LoadRunner and IBM Rational Performance Tester. If we are looking for powerful open source load testing tools, JMeter is the best option. In this chapter, we will consider JMeter as the load testing tool.

Preparing load testing scripts

As discussed earlier, load testing is conducted using load testing tools. Irrespective of any load testing tool, load testing scripts are required to run specific load testing scenarios. The syntax for writing load testing scripts will vary from one tool to the other but the concept remains the same. In this section, we will talk about some of the best practices for writing load testing scripts. We will consider JMeter as the load testing tool for understanding the concepts and best practices.

Load testing scripts are written with a sequence of operations that are performed by multiple concurrent threads. Here are some of the key parameters for JMeter load testing scripts that should be configured correctly to make load testing more realistic:

- **Concurrent threads**: This parameter controls how many concurrent executions of the load testing operations should be performed. This parameter should be configured carefully. This parameter also depends upon the machine from which we are running the load test. If it is configured to a very high value, the JMeter instance may go out of memory or it may not give accurate load testing results. To test a very high amount of concurrent threads, it is advisable to run load tests through multiple machines.

- **Loop count / duration**: This parameter defines how many times or for how much time concurrent executions should happen. In order to get accurate results, load tests should be executed for a longer duration. It should not be less than 30 minutes unless there is a specific need.

- **The ramp-up period**: This parameter controls the period within which the load testing tool will create a maximum number of concurrent threads configured in the script. For example, if a portal is expected to have 2000 concurrent users during pick time, all 2000 users will not start accessing the portal at the same time. They will start accessing the portal one by one and at a certain point in time all 2000 users will be accessing the Portal. So, here the time interval within which the number concurrent users reach from zero to 2000 is the ramp-up period. If it is configured incorrectly, it may give unrealistic load test results.

- **The think time**: This parameter controls the wait time between two operations of the load testing script. Let's take an example of a user accessing a portal. He/she will first log in to the portal, then access page X and then access page Y, and so on. The user will take some time after logging in and before accessing page X. This time is called the **think time**. This parameter should be configured properly to generate a realistic load on the system. If it is configured to a very low value, the portal will be flooded with a number of requests. And it will not be a realistic scenario.

Apart from the aforementioned parameters, there are some of the Liferay-specific best practices that should be followed while writing test scripts. They are as follows:

- Login is one of the costliest operations in Liferay Portal. It is recommended to write realistic test scenarios where the user first signs in and then performs various operations and finally signs out.

- JMeter provides a way to read CSV- or XLS-based inputs to perform any operations. It is recommended to create a number of dummy users in Liferay Portal and perform a load test with those dummy users. If load tests are performed with a single user, it will not generate a realistic load.

- JMeter instances should be configured on the machine that is in the same network as Portal. If JMeter instances are not part of same network as Portal, the load test may give inaccurate results because of varying Internet speed. The purpose of load testing is not to determine the bottleneck of a network between the user and server. Hence, it is recommended to run load tests from the same network.

Setting up the load testing environment

Load testing is normally performed after functional testing is done. Once we are ready with load testing scripts, the next step is to set up the load testing environment. The load testing environment should be of one that is in production such as hardware and deployment configuration. As the purpose of load testing is to verify if the system passes performance expectation with the pick time load, load testing and tuning should be done on a production-like environment. All necessary resource monitoring tools should be installed and configured. Enough space should be allocated for storing various monitoring logfiles.

JMeter should be set up on separate machines with enough memory and CPU capacity. If the number of concurrent users is too high, it is recommended to run load tests from multiple machines. In general, we can run load tests with around 300 concurrent users from a machine with 2 GB RAM allocated to the JMeter application.

Conducting load tests

Load testing is an iterative exercise. It is highly integrated with the resource monitoring and performance tuning exercise. The following diagram explains the iterative process of conducting load tests:

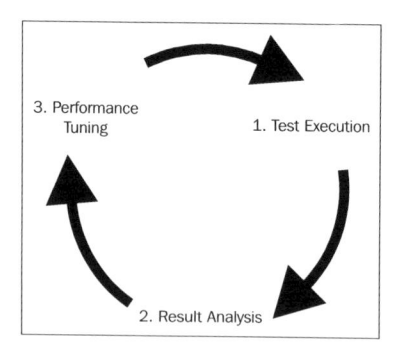

As shown in the diagram, the first step is to execute the load test and monitor resources. The second step is to analyze the load test results and the resource monitoring data. Based on the analysis, necessary changes in the environment, source code or load testing scripts should be produced and then again the same cycle should be followed until expected performance targets are achieved.

As mentioned earlier, JMeter provides good GUI-based reporting plugins. Using many reporting plugins can slow down JMeter. Hence, it is recommended to use only those reports that are necessary. Most of the time, we would like to capture average response time, response time of 90 percent requests, throughput, error percentage, and so on. These results can be captured using the aggregate report of JMeter.

In the next section we will talk about the resource monitoring and performance tuning steps in detail.

Resource monitoring and performance tuning

One of the most important steps in a load testing exercise is resource monitoring and performance tuning. In *Chapter 1, Architectural Best Practices*, we looked at the reference architecture of a Liferay-Portal-based solution. In the reference architecture, we have used different components to build a high performing portal solution. Performance of the solution depends upon each of the components of reference architecture. Hence, during a load test, monitoring the performance of every component is required. In this section, we will talk about resource monitoring of various components. We will also learn about how to read resource monitoring data and tune the system.

Liferay Portal server – monitoring and tuning

As we know, Liferay Portal runs on an application server. In our reference architecture, we used Tomcat as the application server. There are many resources of Liferay Portal, such as JVM, thread pool, or cache engine, which can affect the overall performance of the system. It is required to closely monitor these resources during a load test to optimize the performance. Before we proceed with individual resource monitoring and tuning, let's learn about some of the key monitoring tools and how to configure them with Liferay Portal.

JConsole

JConsole is a GUI-based tool for monitoring applications launched using JVM. It is a **Java Management Extension (JMX)** compliant tool. It can be used to monitor JVM Heap, CPU usage, garbage collection, threads, and JMX-enabled beans. It is a very lightweight tool and adds a minor overhead on the running application. The JConsole utility comes as a part of Oracle JDK installation. It can connect to any remote or local Java-based applications. In order to connect JConsole with a remote application, the JMX port on the remote JVM has to be configured. Let's learn how to configure our Liferay Portal nodes to enable JConsole-based monitoring:

1. Stop both the Liferay Portal nodes if they are running.

Load Testing and Performance Tuning

2. Now add the following environment variable in the `node-01\liferay-portal-6.1.1-ce-ga2\ tomcat-7.0.27\bin\setEnv.bat` file of `liferay-node-01`:

   `set CATALINA_OPTS=-Dcom.sun.management.jmxremote -Dcom.sun.management.jmxremote.port=9999 -Dcom.sun.management.jmxremote.ssl=false -Dcom.sun.management.jmxremote.authenticate=false`

   > If the Liferay Portal server is deployed on a Linux- or Unix-based environment, the same changes need to be done in the `setEnv.sh` file.

3. Apply the same changes as mentioned in step 2 on `liferay-node-02`.
4. Restart the two Liferay Portal nodes.
5. Now from the command prompt run the `jconsole` command from the `<JAVA_HOME>\bin` directory.
6. The system will show a connection dialog box, as shown in the following screenshot:

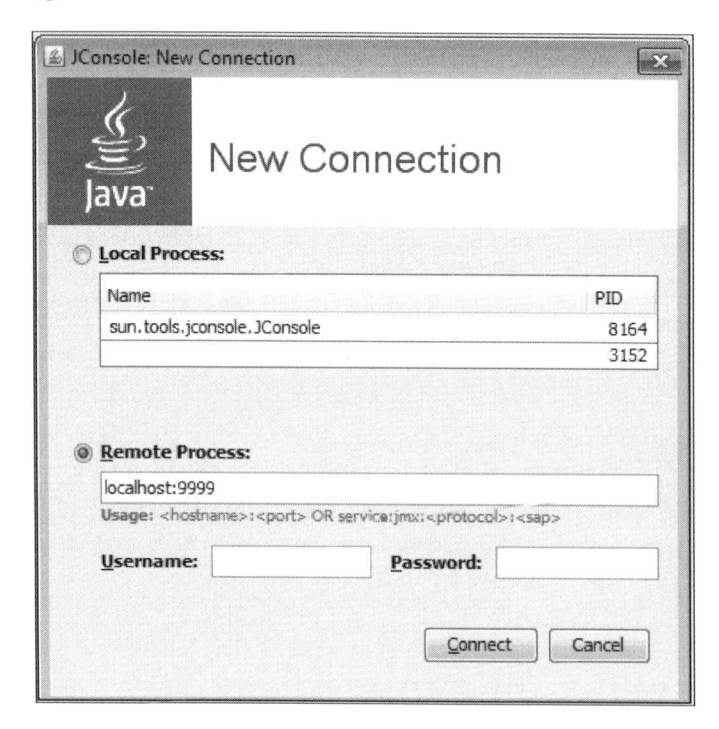

   JConsole: New Connection

   Local Process:

Name	PID
sun.tools.jconsole.JConsole	8164
	3152

   Remote Process:

   `localhost:9999`

   Usage: `<hostname>:<port>` OR `service:jmx:<protocol>:<sap>`

   Username: **Password:**

   [Connect]   [Cancel]

7. Enter the values in the **Remote Process** field as shown in the preceding screenshot and then press **Connect**. The system will open the **Overview** tab.

[112]

In the startup configuration file of the Liferay Portal Tomcat server, we enabled JMX-based monitoring and configured the JMX port. We will talk about how to read and analyze monitoring output in the following sections.

VisualVM

VisualVM is an open source resource monitoring tool for Java. It is actually considered as the next generation of monitoring tools as compared to the lightweight JConsole. VisualVM is included as part of the Oracle JDK installation. It is implemented using the plugin-based architecture, hence, it allows additional plugins for resource monitoring. JConsole can also be used as one of the plugins of VisualVM. VisualVM also includes profiling capabilities. VisualVM allows taking snapshots of monitoring data at any time. This enables us to compare application states at certain events. Similar to JConsole, VisualVM also allows us to connect to local as well as remote Java applications. To connect VisualVM with a remote Liferay Portal Tomcat server, we will need to enable the JMX port. We learned how to enable the JMX port in the previous section. Let's learn how to connect VisualVM with the Liferay Portal Tomcat server.

1. From the command prompt run the following command to start VisualVM:

   `<JDK_HOME>/bin/jvisualvm`

2. The system will open the VisualVM application. Now click on **File | Add JMX Connection...**. The system will open a dialog box as shown in the following screenshot:

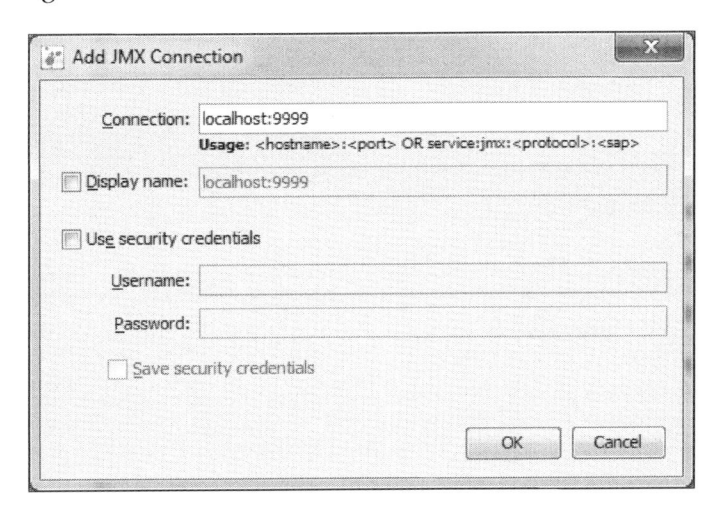

3. Enter the value in the **Connection** test field as shown in the screenshot and then click on the **OK** button.
4. Now from the **Applications** section, double-click on **Local | localhost:9999**.
5. On the right tab view, the system will add a new tab and open the **Overview** subtab.

JVM – monitoring and tuning

We learned how to configure the Liferay Portal server with JConsole and VisualVM. Both of these tools can be used to monitor Liferay Portal JVM. In *Chapter 3, Configuration Best Practices*, we learned how to configure Liferay Portal JVM parameters. We also learned the recommended JVM parameters for the Liferay Portal server. In most cases, the recommended parameters will work well. But there is scope to optimize them according to the developed solution during load testing. The most important areas that need close monitoring during a load test are heap memory and garbage collection. JConsole's **Memory** tab (as shown in the following screenshot) allows us to closely monitor the heap memory and garbage collection activities of the Liferay Portal server:

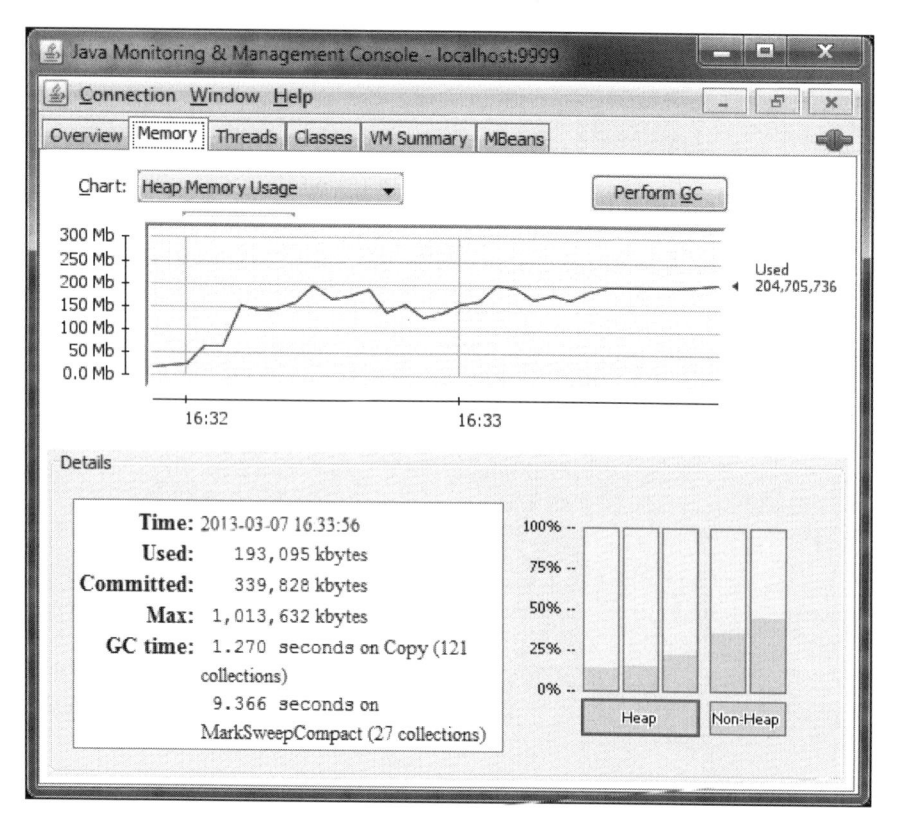

JVM divides heap memory into multiple regions or memory pools. Objects are moved from one pool to the other after garbage collection. Before we talk about what should be monitored on JConsole's **Memory** tab, let's briefly understand heap memory pools:

- **The Eden space**: When an object is created, it will occupy memory space in this pool.
- **The Survivor space**: When the objects that are stored in the Eden space survive at least one garbage collection, they are moved to the Survivor space.
- **The Tenured space** (old generation): When the objects stay in the Survivor space for some time they are then moved to the Tenured Space.
- **Permanent generation space**: This space mainly stores the reflective data of JVM such as class objects. It is also considered as non-heap memory.
- **Code cache**: When HotSpot JVM is used, the **Just-in-time** (**JIT**) compiler stores the compiled classes in this memory pool. It is also considered as non-heap memory.

Objects move from Eden to Survivor and Survivor to Tenured space by garbage collection until they are cleared from the memory. When the garbage collector cleans up objects from the Tenured space, it is called **major garbage collection** (**major GC**). Major garbage collection consumes more resources and also pauses other threads for some time. Frequent major GCs will affect the overall performance of the system. When to go in for major GC or minor GC depends upon the size of these pools. Hence, the size of these memory pools needs to be monitored and optimized during a load test.

As shown in the preceding screenshot, JConsole by default shows a line chart representing the heap memory usage over time. In the bottom-right corner of the **Memory** tab, it shows the memory usage by different memory pools. We can monitor memory usage of individual memory pools by selecting the respective memory pool from the **Chart** drop-down box.

In the **Details** section of the **Memory** tab, JConsole displays the following memory matrices:

- **Used**: This field displayed the memory occupied by all the objects in heap.
- **Committed**: This field displays memory that is occupied by JVM irrespective of whether it is used by objects or not. The JVM may release—time to time—unoccupied memory to the system. The value of this field will be less than or equal to the maximum heap size allocated using the JVM parameter.

- **Max**: This field shows the maximum memory that can be used for memory management.
- **GC Time**: This field shows the total GC time spent by the garbage collector. It shows the time for which other threads were stopped to perform GC.

During monitoring, if we find that the Survivor space is full most of the time, it indicates the size of the young generation (Eden plus Survivor space) is not enough. Because of that it will move more objects into the old generation space. This will increase the possibility of a major GC. Hence, the young generation size should be tuned. The following JVM parameters help in the configuration of the young generation:

- `NewRatio`: This parameter controls the size of the young generation. If the value of this parameter is four, the size of the young generation space (Eden plus Survivor) will be one fourth of the total heap. The rest of the space will be used by the Tenured space.
- `NewSize`: This parameter defines the minimum size of the young generation space.
- `MaxNewSize`: This parameter defines the upper limit of the young generation size.
- `SurvivorRatio`: This parameter defines the ratio of the Survivor and Eden space. If it is configured to six, the Survivor space will be one sixth of the total young generation space.

During a load test, if the trend of the heap memory chart is going upward throughout the load test, it indicates the possibility of a memory leak in the application. In order to conclude this we should run the load test for a longer duration.

During the load test, if it is found that garbage collection is happening again and again, the heap size needs to be tuned. It may be because the young generation is not configured properly or the total heap size is not configured correctly.

During the load test, if it is found that the Permanent generation size is reaching near the maximum Permanent generation size, it is recommended to increase the Permanent generation space.

> JVM tuning in itself is a vast topic. We learned a few of the important JVM tuning options. For more information about garbage collection tuning, please refer to the following URL:
> http://www.kgs.ku.edu/Publications/ancient/f15_snails.html

Tomcat thread – monitoring and tuning

In *Chapter 3, Configuration Best Practices*, we learned to configure the Liferay Portal-Tomcat server with the recommended thread pool configuration. We configured the maximum and minimum size thread pool. The recommended thread pool configuration works in most of the cases, but depending upon the concurrent user requirements, the thread pool configuration should be tuned. In order to fine-tune the thread pool configuration, we will need to monitor the thread pool during load tests. The Tomcat server exposes thread pool statistics using JMX MBeans. JConsole supports monitoring JMX MBeans. Let's learn how to monitor a Tomcat thread pool:

1. Open JConsole and connect JConsole with the respective Liferay Portal node.
2. In JConsole, navigate to the **MBeans** tab.
3. In the **MBeans** tab navigate to **Catalina | Thread Pool** in the tree.
4. In the **Thread Pool** node, you will find AJP and/or HTTP connector nodes. Expand the respective connector and then click on the **Attributes** subnode. The system will show thread pool attributes as shown in the following screenshot:

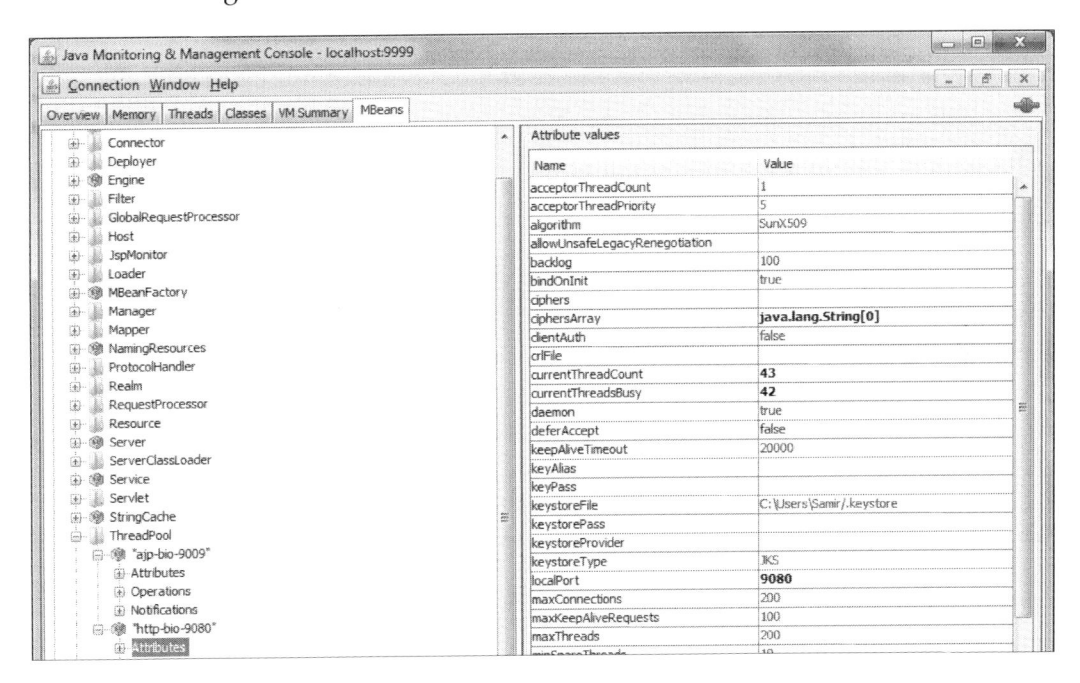

Load Testing and Performance Tuning

As shown in the preceding screenshot, we can get current values of various thread pool attributes. We can use the **Refresh** button to refresh the values. We can keep monitoring the values of thread pool attributes to find out any issues. In order to fine-tune thread pool sizing, the following attributes should be closely monitored:

- `currentThreadCount`: This attribute tell us how many threads are created by the Liferay Portal-Tomcat server. It includes both busy threads and idle threads.
- `currentThreadsBusy`: This attribute tell us how many threads are busy in serving requests.
- `maxThreads`: This attribute tells us how many maximum threads are configured.

During the load test, if it is found that the value of the `currentThreadsBusy` attribute is nearing the `maxThreads` value, it indicates some issue with the thread pool configuration. The issue could be with the `maxThreads` value. In such a situation, the `maxThreads` value should be increased. If the same issue persists even after increasing the `maxThreads` value, further analysis of threads should be done. This can be done by taking the thread dump. We can take the thread dump of the Liferay Portal server through the control panel. We can also monitor individual threads using JConsole. The **Threads** tab of JConsole provides a way to monitor all the threads as shown:

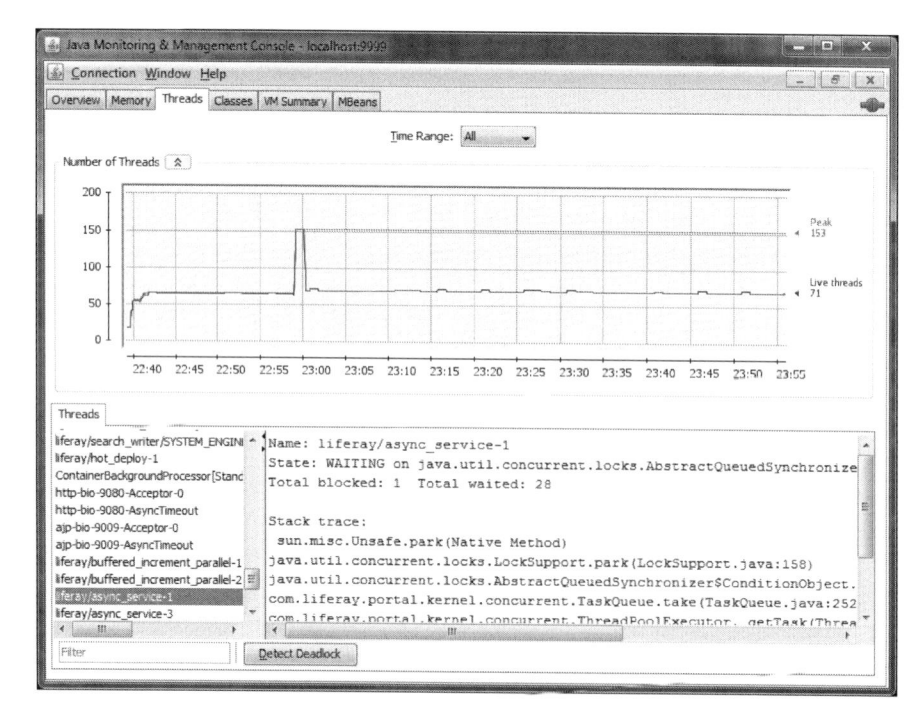

Here, JConsole displays a line chart representing the number of threads over time. It considers all the threads of the Tomcat server and not only thread pool threads;

it also allows the reviewing of the stack trace by individual threads.

During a load test, if it is found that CPU usage of Liferay Portal is very high all the time, one of the reasons could be because of a thread deadlock. Using JConsole we can detect such thread locks. As shown in the preceding screenshot, at any time during the test we can click on the **Detect Deadlock** button to find any thread deadlocks.

During a load test, if it is found that the value of the `currentThreadsBusy` attribute is always very low compare to the value of the `maxThreads` attribute, it indicates that the thread pool might be oversized. We can reduce the thread pool size by modifying the value of the `maxThreads` attribute.

Database connection pool – monitoring and tuning

A database connection pool impacts a lot on the overall performance of the Liferay Portal server. In *Chapter 3, Configuration Best Practices*, we learned how to configure a JNDI-based database connection pool. We learned about the recommended database pool configuration. For most of the Liferay Portal solutions, this configuration works well. But there is always scope for improvement, so it is recommended to monitor the database connection pool during a load test. Database connection pool statistics are exposed using JMX MBeans by the Liferay Portal-Tomcat server. Here are the steps to monitor a database connection pool using JConsole:

1. Open JConsole and connect JConsole with the respective Liferay Portal node.
2. In JConsole, navigate to the **MBeans** tab and then navigate to the **com.mchange.v2.c3p0** node in the MBeans tree.
3. From this node, select a subnode starting with the name **PooledDataSource**.

Load Testing and Performance Tuning

4. Then, select the **Attributes** subnode. The system will display the database connection pool attributes as shown in the following screenshot. Keep refreshing the values of the attribute by using the **Refresh** button at the bottom.

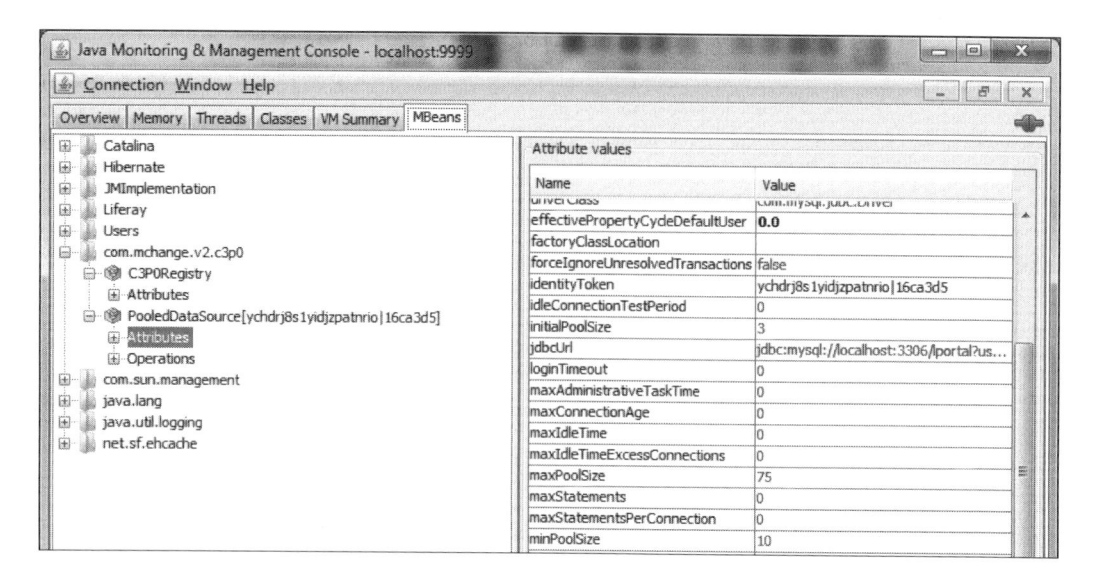

There are many attributes exposed by the database connection pool MBean. The following list outlines the important attributes that should be tracked during a load test:

- `numBusyConnections`: This attribute tells us how many database connections are in use by the Liferay Portal server.

- `maxPoolSize`: This attribute tells us the maximum number of connections that can be created in a database connection pool. This attribute is static and the value of this attribute is controlled by the database connection pool configuration.

- `numConnections`: This attribute tells us how many connections are created in the database connection pool. It includes both busy and idle connections.

During the load test, if it is found that the value of the `numBusyConnections` attribute is always nearing the value of the `maxPoolSize` attribute, it indicates an issue with the database connection pool. It could be because of the undersized database connection pool. If the same issue persists even after increasing the database connection pool size then the issue might be because of open database connections or slow query executions.

Similarly, if the value of the `numBusyConnections` attribute is very low as compared to the value of the `maxPoolSize` attribute, it indicates that the database connection pool is oversized.

Cache – monitoring and tuning

In *Chapter 4, Caching Best Practices*, we spoke about how to provide custom configuration for default Ehcache-based caching. Liferay creates many cache instances for both multi-VM and Hibernate cache managers. Liferay includes the default cache configuration for each cache instance. Depending upon the Portal, requirement-specific cache instances can be tuned to improve performance. Liferay Portal exposes cache information using JMX MBeans. Liferay Portal exposes two types of cache information: one is related to actual cache objects and the other one is for overall cache statistics. During load testing, cache statistics should be monitored. By default, cache statistics are not exposed via JMX MBeans. It is required to enable cache statistics using the Liferay Portal configuration. Here are the steps to enable cache statistics in our setup:

1. Stop both Liferay Portal nodes if they are already running.
2. Now add the following properties in `portal-ext.properties` of the two nodes:

   ```
   #
   # To enable cache statistics for Single VM, Multi VM
   # Cache Managers
   #
   ehcache.statistics.enabled=true
   #
   # To enable cache statistics for Hibernate cache manager
   #
   hibernate.generate_statistics=true
   ```

3. Restart both the Liferay portal nodes.

We enabled cache statistics for both Liferay Portal's cache manager and Hibernate's cache manager. Once cache statistics are enabled, we can monitor cache statistics using JConsole. Here are the steps to monitor the cache using JConsole:

1. Open JConsole and connect JConsole with the Liferay Portal node.
2. In JConsole, navigate to the **MBeans** tab and then expand **net.sf.ehcache** | **CacheStatistics** | **liferay-multi-vm-clustered**.

Under the **liferay-multi-vm-clustered** tree node, we can find all the cache instances as subnodes. Click on the **Attributes** subnode of the specific cache. The system will display cache statistics of the selected cache instance as shown in the following screenshot:

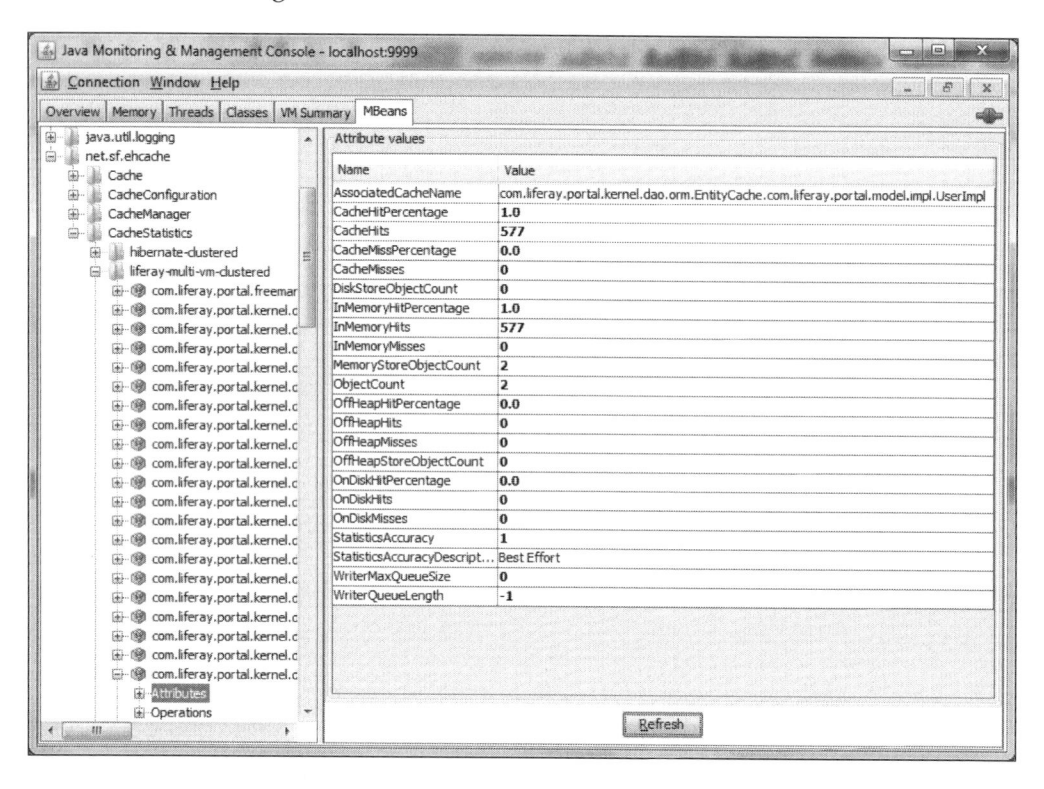

Cache statistics provide information of various attributes, but here are the key attributes that should be monitored during a load test:

- `ObjectCount`: This attribute tells us how many objects there are in the cache.
- `OnDiskHits`: This attribute tells us how many requests are successful in locating objects from a filesystem-based cache. This attribute is useful if we enabled overflow to the disk attribute of the cache instance.
- `InMemoryHits`: This attribute tells us how many requests are successful in retrieving objects from an in-memory cache.
- `CacheHits`: This attribute tells us how many requests are successful in retrieving objects from the cache. It includes both in-memory and disk-based caches.
- `CacheMisses`: This attribute tells us how many requests are unsuccessful in retrieving objects from the cache.

We learned that there are many cache instances in Liferay Portal. It is not possible to monitor every instance during load tests. Hence, cache monitoring is done based on specific performance issues. Depending on the most used functionalities of the Portal, cache instances should be identified and monitoring those cache instances should be done during a load test.

During a load test, if it is found that the value of the `CacheMisses` attribute is very high, it indicates that the cache is undersized. In that case, the size of the cache should be increased.

Apache web server – monitoring and tuning

In our reference architecture, we have used an Apache web server in front of Liferay Portal servers. During a load test, we need to monitor the following resources of the Apache web server.

- CPU and memory
- Worker threads

There are many tools available in the market to monitor CPU and memory consumption of the Apache web server. On a Linux- or Unix-based server, we can simply use the TOP command to monitor CPU and memory consumption. With this option, it will be difficult to monitor resource usage over time. For this kind of monitoring, any SNMP-based monitoring tool can be used. Nagios is one of the most powerful open source monitoring tools. The Apache web server can be configured with Nagios to monitor CPU and memory consumption. With the use of Nagios, we can monitor worker threads as well.

The Apache web server also comes up with a simple monitoring module called `mod_status`. It can be used to monitor worker threads. The following are the steps to enable this tool:

1. Locate the `httpd.conf` file in the `<APACHE_HOME>/conf` directory on the Apache web server and add the following configuration into it:

    ```
    LoadModule status_module modules/mod_status.so
    ExtendedStatus On
    <location /server-status>
      SetHandler server-status
      Order allow,deny
      Allow from all
    </location>
    ```

2. Restart the Apache web server.
3. From the browser, access `http://localhost/server-status`.

We enabled the `mod_status` module and configured the server's status page. The server status page provides the following monitoring statistics:

- The number of on-going requests
- The number of idle worker threads
- Process details
- The total access requests
- The number of requests served per second

During a load test, if it is found that most of the time there are no idle workers and requests are not going through, it is recommended to resize Apache threads / max client configuration. If the problem still persists, requests might not be processed because the Liferay Portal server is taking more time to respond. If the memory usage is consistently high, it is recommended to reduce the Apache thread / max client pool size.

Monitoring the database server

Liferay Portal is database agnostic. We can configure any JDBC-supported database server with the Liferay Portal server. In our reference architecture, we have used MySQL. Most of the database products provide their own monitoring and tuning tools. In this section we will discuss which items should be monitored during load tests.

CPU and memory usage

CPU and memory usage of the database server must be monitored during a load test to find any performance bottlenecks. As discussed in the previous section, the easiest way to monitor CPU and memory is through the TOP command. But it is recommended to configure SNMP-based tools such as Nagios for CPU and memory usage monitoring. There could be multiple reasons of high CPU or memory usage. After the load test, further investigation will be required to find out the root cause of this.

Slow queries

It is very important to identify database queries that are taking more time. It is also important to find out database queries that are executed many times during the load test. Every database product provides one way or an other to get slow queries or the top n queries.

There are multiple reasons for queries being slow. It could be because of improper indexing, improper query logic, or improper database configuration parameters. During a load test, a list of such queries should be identified, and then before the next load test for run, the necessary performance-related changes should be carried out.

Connections

We learned to monitor and tune the database connection pool in the *Database connection pool – monitoring and tuning* section. But that is one side of it. Performance issues may arise because of improper connection configuration at the database server level as well. So it is very important to monitor connections at the database server level. Every database server provides one way or another to monitor a number of open and idle connection objects in the database. During the load test, these statistics must be closely monitored.

Lock monitoring

Database servers use the locking mechanism to support concurrent access. Sometimes heavy database queries lock database objects for a long time. It will slow down the processing of other requests that are dependent on the same objects. It could be one of the causes of a high number of busy connections on the Liferay Portal server. Most of the database products provide lock-monitoring features. During a load test, database locks should be closely monitored.

Monitoring logfiles

We talked about monitoring various resources using tools. But, sometimes, performance bottlenecks are because of errors in some of the components. Hence, as part of the load testing process, all the logfiles should be monitored after the load test. It is recommended to clear all logfiles before starting the load test. Here is a list of logfiles that should be monitored:

- Liferay Portal logfile
- Application server logfile
- Apache web server access logfile
- Apache web server error logfile
- Apache web server `mod_jk` logfile
- Database server error logfile
- Error logfiles of every application-specific integration components

Summary

We learned about the load testing process. We learned how to monitor JVM, the Liferay Portal thread pool, the database connection pool, and so on. We also learned about Apache web server monitoring. We talked about all the key items to be monitored in a database server. With this knowledge anyone can go ahead and conduct load testing and performance tuning exercises.

Index

A

Active Directory tier 10
Advance File System store 16
AlloyUI 94 9
Amazon S3 10
Announcement portlet
  about 69
  scheduler, disabling 69
Apache Benchmark (ab) 108
Apache JMeter 107
Apache Lucene
  about 26
  index storage on SAN 26
  Lucene Index replication, Cluster Link used 27
Apache Solr 27-29, 54
Apache web server
  monitoring 123
  tuning 124
  used, for configuring load balancer 35
Apache web server based software load balancing 32
Apache web server configuration best practices 76
  Apache Web Server MPM configuration 80, 81
  cache header configuration 79, 80
  GZip compression configuration 78
  static content delivery 76, 77
Apache web server MPM configuration 80, 81
Application Server configuration best practices
  about 70
  database connection pool configuration 70, 72
  JSP engine configuration 74, 75
  JVM configuration 72
  thread pool configuration 75
Application tier 9
asset view counter 66
auto login filter 60, 61
auto login hooks
  configuring 63

B

barebone 77
barebone bundle 95
best practices, Ehcache clustering 47
best practices, load balancing 41
BlazeMeter 107
Blogs portlet
  about 68
  scheduler, disabling 68

C

cache control attributes
  eternal 87
  maxElementsInMemory 87
  overflowToDisk 88
  timeToIdleSeconds 87
  using 88
cache header configuration 79, 80
CacheHits attribute
  monitoring 122
cache manager 84
CacheMisses attribute
  monitoring 122
cache replication
  about 44

Ehcache clustering best practices 47
Ehcache configuration, JGroups used 46
Ehcache replication, Cluster Links used 47
Ehcache replication, RMI used 45
cache statistics
  attributes 122
  enabling 121
  monitoring 121
caching
  about 22, 83
  Terracotta, using 89-92
caching architecture 22
caching options, Liferay Portal
  Ehcache replication, Cluster Link used 23
  Ehcache replication, RMI used 22, 23
  Ehcache used 22
  Terracotta used 24
  web resource caching, Varnish used 25, 26
Calendar portlet
  about 67
  scheduler, disabling 67
CAS filter 61
CAS SSO integration 60
CDN
  about 21
  configuring 21
Central Authentication Service (CAS) 61
clustering 31
clustering best practices, Media Library 52
clustering best practices, search engine 56
cluster, Liferay Portal
  configuring 33
Cluster Link
  about 47
  configuring, for search indexes replication 54
  used, for Ehcache replication 23
  used, for Lucene Index replication 27
Cluster Link-based Ehcache replication
  configuring 47
CMIS-based repository 10
CMIS store 17
CMS (Concurrent Mark and Sweep) threads 73
code analysis tools
  CPD 103
  FindBugs 103

PMD 103
SONAR 103
code cache 115
coding best practices 103
Compuware dynaTrace AJAX Edition
  about 100
  URL 100
Concurrent Collector 72
concurrent threads parameter 108
concurrent users 106
configuration settings, Liferay Portal
  about 60
  auto login hooks 63
  counter increment 63
  Direct Servlet Context 64
  Googles blog search ping integration 66
  pingbacks method 65
  plugin repositories 65
  servlet filter configuration 60
  trackbacks method 65
  user session tracker 64
content delivery
  through, web server 21
Content Delivery Network. *See* **CDN**
Content Management Interoperability Services store. *See* **CMIS store**
counter increment
  configuring 63
counter service
  about 63
  configuring 64
CPD tool 103
CSS files
  reducing 96
CSS image sprites
  about 96
  using 96
currentThreadCount attribute
  monitoring 118
currentThreadsBusy attribute
  monitoring 118

D

database 10
database architecture
  about 18

database sharding 19, 20
read/write database 18, 19
database connection pool
  about 119
  attributes 120
  monitoring 119
database connection pool
    configuration 70, 72
Database Repository tier 10
database server
  connections, tuning 125
  CPU and memory usage, monitoring 124
  locking mechanism 125
  monitoring 124
  slow queries, monitoring 124, 125
database sharding 19, 20
Database store 16
defaultCache element 88
deployment sizing approach
  about 12, 13
  example 15
  performance benchmark test 14
  reference hardware 13
Developer Console 92
Direct Servlet Context 64, 65
Document Object Model. *See* DOM
Documents and Media Library architecture
  about 15
  Advance File System store 16
  CMIS store 17
  Database store 16
  File System store 16
  JCR store 17
  S3 store 18
DOM 100
DOM operations usage
  limiting 100
dynamic queries usage
  limiting 101

E

Eden space 115
Ehcache
  about 22
  replicating, Cluster Link used 23
  replicating, RMI used 22, 23
  used, for caching 22
Ehcache clustering best practices 47
Ehcache configuration
  customizing 83-85
Ehcache configuration best practices 86-89
Ehcache configuration, customizing
  Hibernate Ehcache CacheManager 85
  Multi-VM CacheManager 86
  Single-VM CacheManager 86
Ehcache replication
  RMI used 45
eternal attribute 87
everything bundle 95
example Portal solution
  sample performance requisites 15
  sizing calculation 15
examples, servlet filter configuration
  CAS SSO integration 60
  NTLM SSO integration 60
  SharePoint integration 60

F

fault tolerance, reference architecture 11
File System store 16
FindBugs tool 103

G

Garbage Collection
  about 72
  URL 73
Garbage Collectors
  Concurrent Collector 72
  Parallel Collector 72
  Serial Collector 72
Googles blog search ping integration
  about 66
  asset view counter 66
  document ranks, recording 66
  inline permission checks 69
  Lucene Configuration 70
  scheduler configuration 67
  view count, recording 66
GZip 78
GZip compression configuration 78
GZip filter 62

H

hardware load balancer 32
heap memory pools
  code cache 115
  Eden space 115
  ESurvivor space 115
  Permanent generation space 115
  Tenured space 115
Hibernate Ehcache CacheManager 85
high availability, reference architecture 11
HP LoadRunner 108

I

IBM Rational Performance Tester 108
inline permission check 69
InMemoryHits attribute
  monitoring 122

J

Java Content Repository (JCR) 10
Java Content Repository store. *See* JCR store
Java Heap configuration 73
Java Management Extension (JMX) compliant tool 111
JavaScript bundle 94
JavaScript files
  minifying 98
  reducing 94, 95
JavaScript positioning 99
JConsole
  about 111
  memory matrices, displaying 115
JConsole-based monitoring
  enabling 111, 113
JCR store 17
JGroup-based Ehcache replication
  configuring 46
jQuery 94
JSP engine configuration 74, 75
Just-in-time (JIT) compiler 115
JVM 114
JVM Configuration
  about 72
  Garbage Collection 72, 73
  Java Heap configuration 73
JVM parameters
  MaxNewSize 116
  NewRatio 116
  NewSize 116
  SurvivorRatio 116
JVM tuning 116

L

LDAP integration
  about 68
  scheduler, disabling 68
least recently used (LRU) object 87
Liferay
  about 7
  Announcement portlet 69
  barebone bundle 95
  Blogs portlet 68
  Calendar portlet 67
  everything bundle 95
  LDAP integration 68
  Media Library portlet 69
  Message board portlet 68
  Web Content portlet 68
Liferay caching API
  about 102
  using 102, 103
Liferay Portal
  Apache Web Server configuration best practices 76
  Application Server configuration best practices 70
  caching architecture 22
  configuration settings 60
  configuring, with Solr 54
  database architecture 18
  deployment sizing approach 12
  Documents and Media Library architecture 15
  portlet development best practices 101
  reference architecture 7
  search architecture 26
  search integration options 26
  static content delivery 20
  UI best practices 93
Liferay Portal cluster
  configuring 32, 33

Liferay Portal cluster configuration
  about 41
  cache replication 44
  Media Library 48
  Quartz scheduler configuration 56
  search engine configuration 53
  session replication 42
Liferay Portal nodes
  setting up 33, 34
Liferay Portal server
  cluster, configuring 32, 33
  monitoring 111
  tuning 111
Liferay-specific best practices, test scripts 109
load balancer configuration
  Apache Web Server used 35
  mod_jk module used 35-37
  mod_proxy_ajp used 37, 38
  mod_proxy_http used 39, 40
load balancing
  about 32
  best practices 41
  levels 32
load testing
  about 106
  performing 110
  requisites 106
load testing environment
  setting up 110
load testing requisites
  capturing 106
  concurrent users 106
  response time 106
  TPS(throughput) 107
load testing scripts
  concurrent threads 108
  loop count / duration 108
  preparing 108
  ramp-up period 109
  the think time 109
load testing tools
  Apache Benchmark (ab) 108
  Apache JMeter 107
  BlazeMeter 107
  selecting 107
load tests
  conducting 110
lock-monitoring features 125
logfiles
  Apache web server access logfile 125
  Apache web server error logfile 125
  Apache web server mod_jk logfile 125
  Application server logfile 125
  Database server error logfile 125
  Error logfiles 125
  Liferay Portal logfile 125
  monitoring 125
loop count / duration parameter 108
Lucene
  configuring, for storing index files 53
Lucene Configuration 70

M

major garbage collection (major GC) 115
maxElementsInMemory attribute 87
MaxNewSize parameter 116
maxPoolSize attribute 120
maxThreads attribute
  monitoring 118
Media Library 48
Media Library configuration
  about 48
  clustering best practices 52
  database storage, DBStore used 52
  database storage, JCR store used 49-52
  network file storage, Advanced File System store used 48
Media Library portlet
  about 69
  scheduler, disabling 69
Media Repository tier 10
Message Board portlet
  about 68
  scheduler, disabling 68
minification 98
mod_jk module
  used, for configuring load balancer 35-37
mod_proxy_ajp module
  used, for configuring load balancer 37, 38
mod_proxy_http module
  used, for configuring load balancer 39, 40
mod_status module 124

monitoring tools
  cache 121
  database connection pool 119
  JConsole 111
  JVM 114
  Tomcat thread 117
  VisualVM 113
MPM
  about 80
  event option 80
  options 80
  prefork option 80
  worker option 80
Multi-VM CacheManager 86

N

Nagios 123
Networking tier 9
NewRatio parameter 116
NewSize parameter 116
NTLM SSO filter 61
NTLM SSO integration 60
numBusyConnections attribute 120
numConnections attribute 120

O

ObjectCount attribute
  monitoring 122
OnDiskHits attribute
  monitoring 122
OpenAM 61
OpenSSO filter 61
overflowToDisk attribute 88

P

PageSpeed
  about 100
  URL 100
Parallel Collector 72
peak load 106
performance benchmark test 14
performance, reference architecture 11
performance tuning
  about 111
  Apache web server 123

Liferay Portal server 111
Permanent generation space 115
pingbacks 65
ping service 66
plugin repositories 65
PMD tool 103
portlet development best practices
  about 101
  coding best practices 103
  dynamic queries usage, limiting 101
  Liferay caching API 102, 103
Presentation tier 9

Q

Quartz scheduler configuration 56, 57

R

ramp-up period parameter 109
read/write database 18, 19
reference architecture
  about 7
  Active Directory tier 10
  Application tier 9
  characteristics 10
  Database Repository tier 10
  Media Repository tier 10
  Networking tier 9
  Presentation tier 9
  Search Repository tier 10
  Web tier 9
reference architecture characteristics
  about 10
  fault tolerance 11
  high availability 11
  performance 11
  scalability 11
  security 11
reference hardware 13
resource monitoring
  about 111
  Apache web server 123
  database server 124
  Liferay Portal server 111
  logfiles 125
response time 106

RMI-based replication
  working 45
RMI (Remote Method Invocation)
  about 45
  used, for Ehcache replication 22, 23

S

S3 store 18
SAN 10
scalability, reference architecture 11
scheduler configuration 67
search architecture 26
search engine configuration
  about 53
  Apache Solr search engine, using 54, 55
  clustering best practices 56
  Lucene index replication, Cluster
      Link used 54
  Lucene index storage, on network
      storage 53
search integration options
  Apache Lucene 26
  Apache Solr 27
Search Repository tier 10
security, reference architecture 11
Serial Collector 72
Service Builder 101
servlet filter configuration
  about 60
  examples 60
servlet filters
  auto login filter 60
  CAS filter 61
  GZip filter 62
  NTLM SSO filter 61
  OpenSSO filter 61
  SharePoint filter 62
  Strip filter 62
  ValidHtml filter 63
session replication
  about 42
  configuring 42, 44
SharePoint filter 62
SharePoint integration 60
Single-VM CacheManager 86
sizing 12

SONAR tool 103
sprite image 97
static content delivery
  about 20, 76
  CDN 21
  configuring, through Apache Web
      Server 76, 77
  content delivery, through web server 21
Storage Area Network. See SAN
Strip filter 62
SurvivorRatio parameter 116
Survivor space 115

T

Tenured space 115
Terracotta
  Developer Console 92
  downloading 89
  installing 89
  used, for caching 24, 89, 91, 92
Terracotta community edition
  URL 89
the think time parameter 109
thread pool attributes
  currentThreadCount 118
  currentThreadsBusy 118
  maxThreads 118
  monitoring 118
thread pool configuration 75
timeToIdleSeconds attribute 87
Tomcat thread
  monitoring 117, 118
  tuning 118
trackbacks 65
Transactions per second (throughput) 107

U

UI best practices
  about 93
  CSS files, reducing 96
  CSS image sprites, using 96-98
  DOM operations usage, limiting 100
  JavaScript files, minifying 98
  JavaScript files, reducing 94, 95
  JavaScript positioning 99

web page performance, analyzing with
    tools 100
user session tracker
  configuring 64

V

ValidHtml filter 63
Varnish
  used, for web resource caching 25, 26
VisualVM
  about 113
  connecting, with Liferay Portal Tomcat
    server 113

W

web application accelerators 25
Web Content portlet
  about 68
  scheduler, disabling 68
web page performance
  analyzing, tools used 100
web resource caching
  Varnish used 25, 26
Web tier 9

Y

YSlow
  about 100
  URL 100
YUI 94

Thank you for buying
Liferay Portal Performance Best Practices

About Packt Publishing

Packt, pronounced 'packed', published its first book "*Mastering phpMyAdmin for Effective MySQL Management*" in April 2004 and subsequently continued to specialize in publishing highly focused books on specific technologies and solutions.

Our books and publications share the experiences of your fellow IT professionals in adapting and customizing today's systems, applications, and frameworks. Our solution based books give you the knowledge and power to customize the software and technologies you're using to get the job done. Packt books are more specific and less general than the IT books you have seen in the past. Our unique business model allows us to bring you more focused information, giving you more of what you need to know, and less of what you don't.

Packt is a modern, yet unique publishing company, which focuses on producing quality, cutting-edge books for communities of developers, administrators, and newbies alike. For more information, please visit our website: www.packtpub.com.

About Packt Open Source

In 2010, Packt launched two new brands, Packt Open Source and Packt Enterprise, in order to continue its focus on specialization. This book is part of the Packt Open Source brand, home to books published on software built around Open Source licences, and offering information to anybody from advanced developers to budding web designers. The Open Source brand also runs Packt's Open Source Royalty Scheme, by which Packt gives a royalty to each Open Source project about whose software a book is sold.

Writing for Packt

We welcome all inquiries from people who are interested in authoring. Book proposals should be sent to author@packtpub.com. If your book idea is still at an early stage and you would like to discuss it first before writing a formal book proposal, contact us; one of our commissioning editors will get in touch with you.

We're not just looking for published authors; if you have strong technical skills but no writing experience, our experienced editors can help you develop a writing career, or simply get some additional reward for your expertise.

[PACKT] open source
community experience distilled
PUBLISHING

Instant Liferay Portal 6 Starter

ISBN: 978-1-78216-966-6   Paperback: 54 pages

Create your portal with Liferay and learn its concepts on the go!

1. Learn something new in an Instant! A short, fast, and focused guide delivering immediate results
2. Get acquainted with Liferay's interface
3. Learn the core concepts and terms of Liferay

Liferay User Interface Development

ISBN: 978-1-84951-262-6   Paperback: 388 pages

Develop a powerful and rich user interface with Liferay Portal 6.0

1. Design usable and great-looking user interfaces for Liferay Portals
2. Get familiar with major theme development tools to help you create a striking new look for your Liferay Portal
3. Learn the techniques and tools to help you improve the look and feel of any Liferay Portal

Please check **www.PacktPub.com** for information on our titles

Liferay Portal Systems Development

ISBN: 978-1-84951-598-6 Paperback: 546 pages

Build dynamic, content-rich, and social systems on top of Liferay

1. Use Liferay tools (CMS, WCM, collaborative API, and social API) to create your own Web sites and WAP sites with hands-on examples
2. Customize Liferay portal using JSR-286 portlets, hooks, themes, layout templates, webs plugins, and diverse portlet bridges
3. Build your own websites with kernel features such as indexing, workflow, staging, scheduling, messaging, polling, tracking, auditing, reporting, and more

Liferay Beginner's Guide

ISBN: 978-1-84951-700-3 Paperback: 396 pages

Quick and easy techniques to build, deploy, and maintain your own Liferay Portal

1. Detailed steps for installing Liferay Portal and getting it running, for people with no prior experience of building portals
2. Follow the example of building a neighbourhood site with preinstalled portlets and custom portlets
3. Create your own communities, organizations and user groups, and learn how to add users to them

Please check www.PacktPub.com for information on our titles

Printed in Great Britain
by Amazon.co.uk, Ltd.,
Marston Gate.